Hope this peaks
your interest in
history

Stan Russo

THE 50 MOST SIGNIFICANT INDIVIDUALS IN RECORDED HISTORY:

A RANK IN DESCENDING ORDER

STAN RUSSO

-Inklings Press-

ISBN: 0-9759129-9-2

Copyright © 2005 by Stan Russo

Published by:

Inklings Press
2 N. Lincoln Ridge Dr. #521
Madison, WI 53719
USA

www.inklings.com

This title is printed simultaneously in the United States and the United Kingdom by Lightning Source Inc.

Discounts are available for books bought in bulk for educational or promotional purposes. Please contact the publisher for more details.

Special Thanks To:

Chris Costa

for editing, reading and putting up with it all

Dan Norder

for giving me the opportunity to get this in print

Julian A. Duran Jr.

for designing a fantastic front and back cover

and

Bruce Lamont

for helping to plant the idea

INTRODUCTION

What defines significance? There is no precise mathematical equation to arrive at a quantitative value, leading toward the presence of subjectivity when discussing significance. It is a constantly adapting entity, contingent upon an ever-changing world. The standard definition, having a major effect upon, does specifically apply here, albeit in a subjective state. Two vital factors of significance however, are Society and Era.

Within differing societies the significance of an individual's contribution varies according to the guiding principles of a specific society or civilization. A culture deeply rooted in religious beliefs and rituals might fail to recognize scientific and technological discoveries and the individuals who promote such theories and information. The opposite also applies in that a civilization that encourages and embraces scientific innovations may devalue religion and the creators and or suppliers of theological doctrine.

As with cultural and societal opinions affecting the scope of individual significance, different historical time periods also play a vital role. Over the course of recorded history chronological eras appear to flow in a cyclical motion with regards to significance. At times religious values dominated thought, which in turn led toward glorious ages of scientific discovery, eventually evolving into a pseudo harmonious mixture where both religion and science could exist mutually. One day this flow may venture full circle to begin the cyclical process anew. Only time will tell.

Despite the fact that this is a subjective list, it is not based upon a designated mathematical formula. I found it almost impossible to ascertain a person's value to arrive at a precise analysis using a numerical method. Quantifying significance is an exercise in futility, yet there are at the very least certain factors that aided placement. The easiest way to explain significance as it relates to this work would be a combination of individual influence and importance, with respect to that individual's contribution, while taking into account an overall relative time frame. The time frame used as a starting point in continued recorded history shall be designated as 3200 B.C.

Using the year 3200 B.C as our historical starting point, appearing as the earliest continued record of historical data, in the newly merged civilization of Egypt, there still remains inconsistent information pertaining to certain individuals viewed as historic. For a person to garner a spot on this list there must have been verifiable and logical proof that the specific person existed, based on all known information currently available. Four individuals, who would have placed highly upon this list, must therefore be disqualified. There are also four inventions, evidently created by human individuals, that history has not been able to establish authorship of. These four individuals would also have placed highly on this list, perhaps holding the top four spots as these pre-historic creations revolutionized the world forever.

The four identified individuals are, the Persian prophet Zoroaster, the Biblical patriarch Abraham, the Biblical leader of the Jews Moses and the blind Greek poet Homer. Zoroaster has been credited with both the creation of monotheism and the invention of democracy, yet inconsistent dates of his birth, ranging from mid 7th century B.C. to 5500 B.C., lead toward the conclusion that fact has been merged with folklore. Only one source documents the life of Abraham, the Old Testament of the Bible. In a time period and region where history was recorded by various Semitic tribes and empires, a man who lived 175 years single-handedly creating monotheism, according to Biblical legend, would surely have been written about or referenced by other written or oral sources prior to the Bible. In the case of Moses there is no denying that someone led the enslaved Jews out of Egypt yet the myriad of miracles attributed to Moses creates doubt among those who can see path mere faith, while questions arise as to the true past of Moses, generating further uncertainty as to his possible existence. Homer gave birth to Western literature, yet the general consensus among historians is that Homer, or the Homeric poetry, was not the work of one singular person.

The four major inventions or creations that have altered the course of history are the production of fire, the incline plane, written communication and the wheel. Fire has existed throughout history, yet man-made production of fire has been theorized as occurring around 500,000 B.C. The incline plane is the oldest of the six basic machines, created approximately 2 and a half million years ago. The incline plane allowed groups of people to move an object from a lower elevation to a higher one, thereby minimizing necessary human power. The next two, written communication and the wheel occurred far later in history, around the 4th millennium B.C., are equally comparable to the first two innovations. Behind these miraculous discoveries one man had to be at the heart of their conception, whether it was originating the idea or becoming the first to actually create or produce these inventions. As it is not specifically known who these men were then it is impossible to include them within this list.

The main focus of this list is to provide perspective into the lives and histories of individuals that may otherwise not be known. The reason for the subjective ranking is to foster debate, while offering another temporal and societal opinion regarding the value of significance. That is the key item that should be remembered when evaluating this list; it is subjective, yet I have tried my best to remove all cultural, societal, religious and ethnic biases. Judging each individual along the earlier guidelines I was able to arrange these 50 people in a numerical rank, descending from 50 to 1. Over 500 people were on this list at one time and eliminations were increasingly harder as the work neared completion. I only hope that knowledge is gained and ultimately continued as a result of this work.

50

SIMON DE MONTFORT IV

In 1215 A.D. one of the most important documents in history was signed, the Magna Carta. It would be almost 50 years before that document's basic goal, recognizing the rights of the citizenry, despite emphasizing baronial nobility over commoner, was implemented when a French born English noble-man organized the first Parliament in 1265. Parliament served as the precursor for modern Western democracy. The exact date of Simon De Montfort's birth is speculated at approximately 1208, born into an aristocratic family, the third of four sons. Young Simon was orphaned at 13, with the death of his father, a noted warrior known as Simon the Crusader, coming in 1218 on the field of battle and his mother in 1221. The death of his parents initiated Simon's studies in the art of fighting and becoming a Knight. A claim to the English Earldom of Leicester was split between Simon's grandmother and great-aunt, yet in 1227 English King Henry III denied a petition for the inheritance of the Earldom of Leicester to the Montfort family. Simon would later forfeit his rights to any inherited lands in France for the sole possession of any claims to familial lands in England, and in 1230 Simon traveled to England in pursuit of regaining what was his birth-right.

Through a masterful act of political diplomacy, which would eventually transfer over to the battlefield, Simon acquired the Earldom in August of 1231. Simon would go on to become one of Henry III's most trusted advisors and married Eleanor, the King's widowed sister in 1238. Simon's battle prowess displayed itself on the 1240 crusade in Palestine. He was later called upon in 1248 to halt the feudal wars against English authority in Gascony, France. By 1258 Simon had advanced into the role as leader of the baronial opposition to Henry III. In 1261 the barons agreed to an unfavorable compromise with Henry III prompting Simon to leave England. The following year Henry III annulled his provisions to the barons, forcing Simon to return to England in 1263 to take up arms against Henry III. Suffering from a broken leg Simon led the barons to a victory over Henry III and his Royal forces in 1264 at Lewes, England. Due to this victory Simon De Montfort had become virtual ruler of England. The following year Simon set up the first Parliament inviting representatives that included non-nobles. As a result the English barons turned on Simon and reconciled with Henry III. The barons' original impetus was to obtain a voice in the economic and political advancements of their country, yet they betrayed Simon due to his allegiance to the commoners of the shires and boroughs. That same year the Royal forces defeated and killed Simon ending his short-lived reign as King of England, yet leaving his legacy intact.

English Parliament has remained as one of the oldest sustaining bodies of law in Europe, serving as the ideal for almost all modern Western European ruling institutions. Such institutions, most notably in Western Europe and the United States of America, would help establish democracy as the pre-eminent political system throughout the world. Parliament, or the current Congress in the United States, allows issues to be heard by governing bodies, which directly affects the community yet might be somewhat overlooked by those in power. It also helps to establish a system of checks and balances as individual representatives must abide by their oath to improve and care for the welfare of those who have a direct say in the voting process. In the ideal case this prevents officials from ignoring or diverting attention away from the problems of their constituents, as they require their support for re-election. Despite the political abuse of monarchies and aristocracies during the early developmental stages of English Parliament the more important message of equality within representation of the citizenry sustained and allowed Simon's vision to live on.

Simon De Montfort's first Parliament is considered today as the model Parliament. The monarchy could not ignore the rights of the barons as outlined within the Magna Carta, yet what Simon established with his Parliament was the rights of the commoner, in a time when feudalism was still widespread. Simon's efforts eventually led the way toward a transferal of the supreme powers of the monarchy. Despite the fact that only the aristocracy reaped the benefits of Simon's original Parliament, the commoners and workers of the land surely felt a much-needed boost in their morale, leading in an indirect way toward the end of feudalism. The specific ramifications of Simon's Parliament exist today within the United Kingdom and their overall effect has transferred to the rest of the world. Simon De Montfort's goal of a constitutional monarchy rather than merely an aristocratic monarchy led to his eventual betrayal and demise.

49

ERNEST RUTHERFORD

The field of physics has steadily evolved over the course of history, from purely theoretical to an emphasis on observational and empirical research. Physics as a science continues to evolve and advance today with a number of the most important discoveries occurring in the early twentieth century from the meticulous and precise work of Ernest Rutherford. Known as the father of nuclear physics Rutherford was born in Nelson, New Zealand on August 30th, 1871. His academic excellence in mathematics and physics helped him to obtain a scholarship to Nelson College in 1887 and later a scholarship to study at Cambridge University in England. Studying under the acclaimed physicist Joseph John Thomson, who discovered the sub-atomic particle, Rutherford began his experimental work within the newly expanding field of physics, making an impact almost immediately with his meticulous research.

In 1896 Rutherford discovered that X rays caused matter in a gaseous state to conduct electricity, leading to a conclusion resulting from experimental ionization that X rays consisted of particles. In 1898 he identified two distinct radioactive emissions from the mineral element uranium. Rutherford named these emissions alpha and beta rays, as they showed dissimilar properties and used these two emissions as the starting point to explain the true nature of the atom. His identification of alpha and beta ray emissions in 1898 later allowed him to prove that this specific energy was originating from the interior of the individual atom, thus establishing the principle of atomic energy. Since Rutherford's discovery and empirical research, atomic energy has emerged into a field of its own having widespread uses in the fields of medicine, electrical power, transportation as well as perilous purposes in chemical and technological warfare.

Rutherford next experimented with radioactive thorium illustrating a fixed rate of decay transmuting into different elements. The radioactive thorium experimented upon eventually stabilized as an isotope of lead. As a result of this discovery Rutherford began promoting the belief that radioactivity could be utilized to date the Earth. Precise numerical rates of decay from the transmutation of elements led Rutherford to establish this as an atom's 'half-life', a term he coined. The 1905 paper by Rutherford, and assistant Frederick Soddy, dispelled the long held theorem that the atom was indestructible. His idea that radioactivity could be used in a dating process has become a widely used practice. Currently radioactive carbon dating is utilized within numerous scientific fields, most notably geology. For his work on the radioactive decaying of elements Rutherford earned the Nobel Prize, albeit in chemistry rather than physics.

In 1911 Rutherford announced the discovery of the atomic nucleus showing that solid objects consisted of empty space and that an atom's mass or weight was contained within a tiny central positioned nucleus. His 1911 paper, which mathematically displayed the scattering of alpha particles against a gold foil, initiated the necessity to restructure the periodic table of elements. Three years later Rutherford deliberately transmuted an atom from a specific element into the atom of another differing element. By bombarding nitrogen with alpha particles Rutherford was able to produce an emission of hydrogen nuclei. This final monumental achievement is the first recorded example of atomic fission. This breakthrough along with the model of the atom as a miniature solar system, based upon Rutherford's discoveries, helped create another new field of study, nuclear physics.

Rutherford's multiple discoveries and work in the field of physics have produced various realistic applications, yet the name Ernest Rutherford remains less known in the field of physics than that of Albert Einstein and Marie Curie. That would have suited Rutherford just fine. Results were what counted and fame played little or no part in his ambition to expand and further the field of physics, although during his lifetime he received several accolades, winning the Nobel Prize in 1908, Knighted in 1914 and in 1931 Rutherford was made a baron, only six years before an infection of an umbilical hernia led to his death on October 19th, 1937. His insistence on empirical research and precise mathematical equations to explain his data and research has garnered him consideration as the greatest experimental physicist of all time. Ernest Rutherford helped change physics into a multi-faceted field of study and is at least partially responsible for that continuing process today.

14

48

ABU ALI AL-HUSSAIN IBN ABDALLAH IBN SINA

The Dark and the Early Middle Ages were a time of extreme religious fervor as the battle for geographic supremacy was undertaken in all parts of the known world. As a result science, especially medicine, lagged behind military conquests. One man sought to change this trend and attempt to re-establish and advance the medical and scientific principles that had not flourished since the Greek and early Roman Empire. Known by his westernized name Avicenna, Ibn Sina was born in 980 A.D. in Bukhara, Persia, modern day Uzbekistan. His youth was spent accumulating all the knowledge that was available, learning such subjects as philosophy, law, logic, history, linguistics, religion, mathematics and medicine. At the age of seventeen Avicenna's medical prowess had reached such heights that he was called upon to treat the Samanid ruler. After curing his illness Avicenna was rewarded by having been granted full access to the Samanid Royal Library.

He made the most of his reward by expanding his knowledge in all subjects and areas contained within the library. Through his remarkable memory and intelligence Avicenna became the leading authority of medicine and natural sciences, with respected physicians and scientists working under his direction. The death of his father forced Avicenna to retreat from his main work as scholar and take an administrative position to supplant his income. His medical expertise notwithstanding, Avicenna's exceptional knowledge afforded him the rank of political advisor, which he would later become actively involved in the political affairs of the region. Constant political turmoil prompted Avicenna to flee from his position and practice as a wandering surgeon, consulting on matters relating to medicine.

Avicenna is known primarily through the wealth of written information he left behind on a wide array of subjects. It has been estimated that he wrote over 450 manuscripts, of which approximately 250 remain, although that number has been devalued in recent history regarding the authenticity of authorship. By the age of twenty-one he had written his first book on natural philosophy. The two books that Avicenna gained the most notoriety for are *The Book of Healing*, an encyclopedia of natural sciences based upon a mathematical structure, and *The Canon of Medicine*, considered by many to be the most important medical textbook ever written. After suffering imprisonment then eventual release, as well as a self-diagnosed and self-cured outbreak of the colic, Avicenna passed away in 1037 in Hamadan, Persia, modern day Iran.

In his famous work *The Book of Healing*, he dealt with the mathematical applications toward natural sciences. In compiling a virtual almanac mathematics were divided into four distinct topics, arithmetic, geometry, astronomy and music. Addressing natural philosophy and sciences by a mathematical approach was a precursor to the techniques employed by seventeenth century researchers in establishing modern science. The second and more famous book written by Avicenna is *The Canon of Medicine*. Completed during the 1020's his book became the medical authority until the seventeenth century. Within this work Avicenna became the first doctor to identify meningitis and the contagious nature of tuberculosis. Further innovative discoveries included anatomical descriptions of the eye, heart, specific nerves, the spreading of diseases through water and pharmacological methodology. Similar to his mathematical philosophy text, this work was a compendium of prior knowledge on the subject of medicine, which included Avicenna's own personal observational advancements. The book's systematic approach to medicine overshadowed the previous medical texts of its day, remaining as the primary sourcebook in Islamic medicine today.

Entrenched with the belief in the advancement of knowledge, Avicenna has been alternatively described as a Sufi mystic, due to a number of his writings on philosophy, or as an unparalleled medical genius. During Avicenna's time there was no person in his immediate region who was his intellectual superior and there was no subject that he could not master. Avicenna did not rest upon his success as the preeminent scholar, yet rather journeyed to expand that knowledge and assist others in need. His medical expertise may have given him the title of 'Prince of Physicians', yet it is his overall ability to master the known world that has enabled his reputation to endure, making him in an indirect way one of the earliest Renaissance men and the greatest mind of an unstable era.

18

JAMES WATT

Toward the end of the eighteenth century the world would experience a radical change in daily life. Originally occurring in Europe the Industrial Revolution drastically altered production capabilities and increased our technological capacity for expansion and growth. There were a number of inventions that sparked the Industrial Revolution yet one specific invention, or rather an advanced modification on a pre-existing invention, embodied the particular spirit of potential that the Industrial Revolution stood for. One man's inventive genius allowed such progress to occur, that man was James Watt. Born on January 19th, 1736, in the small town of Greenock, Scotland, his father, also James, relocated to Greenock in 1730, after apprenticing as a carpenter. James was home schooled by his mother, possibly overprotective, resulting from the death of their first five children during infancy. James eventually went off to school and excelled in mathematics, but would often spend time in his father's workshop tinkering with the various tools, gathering any and all mechanical information he could. This invaluable knowledge would serve Watt extremely well, leading him on the path to his future career.

Watt relocated to Glasgow in 1754 after the death of his mother, at which time he attempted to find work as a mathematical instrument maker. After a short stint in London Watt returned to Glasgow where he would later find himself at Glasgow University. While there he was asked to repair an atmospheric steam engine. Performing a number of experiments on the steam engine, invented by Thomas Newcomen in 1712, Watt discovered a number of flaws within the framework and structure of the original model. Newcomen's steam engine was not able to sufficiently supply enough steam to run the engine for a continuous period of time. In fact, the Newcomen model would fail after a considerably short usage period. Watt's first improvement to this was the separate condenser in 1765. The separate condenser cooled the steam to create a perfect vacuum, exerting the full power potential of the cooled steam. Watt finally patented his first steam engine employing the separate condenser in 1769. Further advancements to the steam engine followed, including insulating the boiler preventing the loss of heat and changing the straight linear motion of the steam piston to a more efficient circular motion of a drive shaft. These improvements to Newcomen's model and to Watt's own original improved model increased the productivity of the steam engine fourfold. This increase created numerous applications to industry.

In 1774, Watt formed a partnership with Matthew Boulton. This partnership made the Watt steam engine a commercial success. Further inventions followed including the centrifugal steam governor for automatic speed control, the double acting steam engine, a gauge to regulate steam pressure and a letter copying press, one of the earliest photocopiers. These inventions, in commercial endeavors with Boulton, made Watt a financial success, allowing him to focus on his passion, inventing and improving machinery, which would in turn improve daily life. Watt is also responsible for coining the term horsepower and the British Association later gave his name to the unit of electrical power. In 1784 he was elected a Fellow of the Royal Society of Edinburgh. The following year he was elected a Fellow of the Royal Society of London, and in 1806 Watt was awarded an Honorary Doctorate of Law from the University of Glasgow. He continued inventing in later life creating a proportional sculpturing machine, until eventually passing away on August 25th, 1819.

More than any single invention, the Watt steam engine, using the separate condenser, spawned the Industrial Revolution. The output capacity of Watt's engine increased productivity by removing the reliance on manpower, which was often slow and tedious as well as cost ineffective. The steam engine powered railroads, coalmines, textile factories and steamships creating more jobs and the need to move out of an agrarian lifestyle into a mechanized urban setting. This in turn helped create a middle class that increased education, wealth and economic expansion. A better, easier way of life existed for some, while the factory system indirectly accredited to the steam engine had the reverse effect. This new demand for labor included the use of minors who would be exploited until changes were ultimately forced. The Industrial Revolution affected people in variously different ways, yet one fact remains; James Watt's inventive genius for improved and advancing machinery would change the world forever.

22

46

ALARIC

There are times in history when a single event has such a profound effect upon the future course of history that it ranks above certain events, discoveries and or inventions that have impacted the lives of those around it. It is a challenge to measure the worth of an event such as this, in comparison to some of the other major events that immediately altered the world, yet its lasting and overall impression must be included when quantifying worth. The fall of the Roman Empire remains as one of the most important world altering events in the course of human history. At the heart of all this was a warrior named Alaric.

Alaric was born in 370 A.D., on the island of Peuce, near the mouth of the Danube River, currently lying within Romania. Extremely little is known about Alaric's early years, yet it can be easily hypothesized that he was brought up in the ways of barbarian warfare, stressing conquest and survival over education. The earliest record known of Alaric is in 390 A.D. when he was chosen as the leader of the Visigoths, a Germanic barbarian horde employed within the Roman Empire, for the sole purpose of protecting Rome and its territories from other invading barbarian hordes, such as the Vandals or the Huns. Alaric, like many other barbarian leaders, would occasionally turn upon their Roman masters and attack provinces at will. A Vandal General, Flavius Stilicho, also loyal to Rome, was usually there in battle against Alaric, to thwart the Visigoth attempt at conquest. Other times Alaric and his men were bought off, re-swearing their allegiance to Rome. When Western Roman Emperor Honorius murdered Stilicho in 408 A.D., this afforded Alaric the opportunity he long awaited for.

After the death of the only man who consistently could defeat Alaric, his attention was turned toward Rome. He sacked the city twice, in 408 and 409 A.D. Both times a ransom or a bribe was offered for his conditional retreat. Alaric's main goal was to acquire wealth and title, yet once the payments ran out Alaric, without the Vandal Stilicho to stop him, returned to lay siege to Rome. In 410 A.D. Alaric and his barbarians attacked Rome and took control of the city. Some cite a sanctioned attack on Alaric and his followers, by the current Roman Emperor, as the instigation for this third and final attack on Rome. Alaric immediately sought to extend his new realm to Sicily and North Africa, yet uncontrollable weather conditions hindered his plans. Shortly after leading the first group to conquer Rome since 390 B.C., Alaric passed away before returning to Rome.

One of the main elements that arose from the 410 A. D. conquering of Rome was the basic disintegration of the Roman Empire. While it would technically take another sixty-six years for the Roman Empire to officially fall, this event would serve as the precursor. Rome was the greatest Empire the world had ever seen, controlling lands reaching as far as the Western European shores. One such area under its control was Britain. Rome had held Britain since the late 1st century A.D. Once Rome had been sacked in 410, Britain was set free from under the yoke of Roman rule. This pivotal point in European history helped shape the England of the Dark and early Middle Ages, allowing for the assimilation of the Angles and the Saxons, two Germanic tribes who essentially created an entirely new country, which would go onto alter the course of Western European history.

The ambitious conquest of Alaric greatly affected two contemporaries, both of whom are revered in history as far more noteworthy than Alaric, Augustine of Hippo and Attila the Hun. Augustine, considered as one of the three greatest Christian theologians, was a prolific author. His most prominent work, *City of God*, is a sprawling exoneration of Christianity in response to the superstitious impressions of the time that Rome was sacked in response to the abandoning of Paganism. This landmark work became the primary text for the establishment of the Holy Roman Empire during the Dark Ages and their control and suppression of scientific knowledge that kept Europe stagnant for such a long period of time. Attila, the most infamous leader of the Huns, has his legend cemented in the history books for his numerous attacks on Roman provinces. His all out attack on the diminishing Roman Empire in 451 and 452 A.D. might never have occurred if not for the sacking of Rome in 410, which thoroughly demystified an Empire that had previously instilled fear in all foes. The mere conquering of an Empire that had remained intact and unchallenged for the past 800 years is a momentous enough event in the course of history, yet coupled with the future ramifications that resulted, ensures that Alaric rightfully deserves a place upon this list.

THEOPHRASTUS PHILLIPPUS AUREOLUS BOMBAST
von HOHENHEIM

Scientific theory regarding medicine had been accepted as fact due to religious affiliation and divergent opinions were viewed as heretical, with the proponents of these innovative ideas persecuted and often put to death. As a result the progress of medicine was severely impeded until an early 16th century physician chose to rise against the tyranny of the Church and challenge long standing beliefs regarding medicine and medical practices. Known to the world as Paracelsus, he was born of the noble family Bombastus, on May 1st, 1493 in the small town of Einsiedeln outside what is currently Zurich, Switzerland. His mother, originally from Einsiedeln, committed suicide when Paracelsus was only ten, whereupon Paracelsus and his father Wilhelm relocated to Villach, Carinthia in the Austrian Alps. While living in Villach, Wilhelm worked as a teacher in the mining school. Wilhelm was the city physician and was Paracelsus' primary teacher, instructing him in chemistry, medicine, logic and Latin. An intense student for knowledge, Paracelsus would study both metallurgy and alchemy before leaving Villach at the age of fourteen to travel throughout Europe, settling down in Strasburg, Germany in 1526.

Paracelsus was appointed the city physician and the instructor of medicine for the university in Basel, Switzerland, after treating an infected leg of the famous printer Johann Froben. During his stay in Basel Paracelsus began lecturing on the current, yet outdated practices of medicine. After the death of Froben in 1528, Paracelsus was forced to leave Basel due to the controversial nature of his speeches and beliefs regarding the ancient medical practices. The rest of Paracelsus' days were spent traveling and observing the nature of daily life. He would accept an invitation from the Prince of Bavaria to stay in Salzburg after traveling through most of the 1530's, remaining in Salzburg for the rest of his days, eventually dying of natural causes on September 24th, 1541. It is uncertain if the malady of rickets that Paracelsus had during his childhood shortened his life, but it may be easily hypothesized that his death at the young age of forty-eight, only years before Europe would experience a medical revolution, negatively affected his stature in the annals of historical medicine.

Throughout Paracelsus' life the world still wholeheartedly accepted the medical doctrines of the 2nd century doctor Claudius Galen. Paracelsus studied the time honored medical traditions of Galen yet strongly disagreed with the conclusions regarding the inner workings of the human body. Galen's medical determinations had become accepted due to his connections with the Church and as such were above challenge. Paracelsus' main goal was to eliminate the reliance on Galenic medicine, because the advancement of medical knowledge and physiology had become relatively stagnant over the centuries. By straying from the medical doctrines of mysticism and accepted theory that had reigned for the previous millennia he was able to challenge the ancient wisdom and lead the way toward the medical revolution in the 16th century. Through an unwavering determination Paracelsus directly challenged the accepted medical doctrine and was indirectly responsible for paving the way for medical visionaries such as Andreas Vesalius who advanced anatomy, and William Harvey who discovered the true circulatory pathways of blood, both in opposition to Galenic medicine. They and others continued the challenge pioneered by Paracelsus, succeeded where he may have initially failed, yet their triumph results from Paracelsus' initiative and remains the world's gain.

Paracelsus treated such diseases as syphilis, calling upon his background in metallurgy to administer mercury, a remedy that became widely accepted four centuries after his death. Growing up in a mining community, Paracelsus examined diseases connected to that industry, concluding that these diseases arose from the miners inhaling noxious fumes, rather than the prevailing doctrine of evil spirits creating the malady, moving medicine from religious mysticism into reasoned science. He was also the first physician to link the then separate practices of chemistry and medicine. His outright contempt and disdain for textbook learning allowed him to advance medicine, while simultaneously absorbing the main brunt of the elder scholars scorn and criticism for future medical professionals and innovators to succeed where at times he failed. His reliance on empiricism and observation peaked his natural curiosity and an attempt to find a cure for every known disease was undertaken, displaying his passionate spirit. A newborn insight for the advancement of learning was created out of these challenges to established dogma, an advancement that still continues today.

30

44

YUSEF SALAH ED-DIN IBN AYYUB

During the apex of the Middle Ages a dark religious war took place where both parties battled over a geographic territory that symbolized a holy land. In the bloody aftermath of almost 200 years of warfare certain individual participants played a more pivotal role in shaping world history than others. One such man was Yusef Salah Ed-din, known to the Western world as Saladin, born in 1138 in Tekrit, modern day Iraq. Of Kurdish descent, Saladin's father, Ayyub Nejm ed-Din, relocated to Damascus and was given command of an army when Saladin was nine years old. Saladin grew up in Damascus concentrating his efforts on literature and Sunni theology. During 1164 Saladin accompanied his uncle to Egypt along with an army in battle against Jerusalem. During these battles Saladin exhibited himself as an able strategic and military leader, later becoming Vizier, a position generally filled by a prince or a person displaying exceptional ability, of Egypt in 1169. Using his aptitude for strategy Saladin would slowly take over control of Egypt.

Just six years later Saladin would declare himself King of Egypt and Syria in 1175, establishing a foothold in Egypt while strengthening his ties within the Muslim world. Attacks and triumphs in Northern Syria and Iraq would follow. By 1187 Saladin ruled almost the entirety of the Muslim world in the East. With control over so many forces Saladin's main goal was to be fulfilled. On July 4th, 1187 Saladin's forces attacked the Christian held city of Jersualem. By September Saladin had re-gained control of the city once held by the Muslim community before the original crusade in 1099. Christian armies from England, France and Germany, immediately embarked on the third crusade regaining a number of Muslim held fortresses, however, never reached Palestine. Saladin, despite losing most of his strongholds, managed to hold onto Jerusalem, the holy land sought after by the Crusaders. In defeat Saladin had gained an impressive victory. A short-lived peace was agreed upon in 1192 although Saladin would die the following year in Damascus. He left behind the legacy of a masterful and temperate warrior who fought for his people and his religious beliefs.

The capturing of Jerusalem by Saladin in 1187 has a large number of vital implications. Firstly the conquering of Jerusalem unified the Muslim world under one leader who had re-taken and then defended their holy land. The restoration of dignity and honor can directly be seen from the noble efforts of Saladin to reclaim what was taken from his people eighty-eight years earlier merely to exert the power of the Roman Catholic Church. Today Jerusalem remains as a political/ religious center in the ongoing battle for holy supremacy. Lotario Di Segni, crowned Pope Innocent III in 1198 initiated a Fourth Crusade against the Muslims to regain the Christian Holy Land, due to Saladin's military victory a decade earlier. This crusade was indirectly, or perhaps directly responsible for the introduction of papermaking into Europe from the Muslim community, eventually leading toward the scientific revolution of the 15th and 16th centuries.

Continuing effects from Saladin's recapture of Jerusalem include the demise of England's King Richard the Lionhearted, who would be killed in France in 1199, during the Fourth Crusade. This left the running of England to John I, who through his mismanagement and cruelty was forced to sign the Magna Carta by the English barons, setting up what was intended to be an aristocratic monarchy. The Magna Carta laid down the core principles of constitutional democracy and the disregarding of that major document by King Henry III prompted a war in 1264 where King Henry III was defeated and the first session of English Parliament was called by Simon De Montfort to ensure the rights of the commoner.

Through the advent of such traits as bravery, courage, kindness and clemency, Yusef Salah ed-Din ibn Ayyub was directly responsible for restoring the pride of one nation while indirectly helping spawn the evolution of another nation. A comparison to Richard the Lion-Hearted, ruthless and vicious to his conquered captives, puzzled many a historian including celebrated author Sir Walter Scott, who noted that there was a definitive contrast between the two enemies, with Richard displaying the cruelty of a stereotypical Sultan, and Saladin exhibiting all the noble qualities of an English Knight. That disparity still goes unnoticed in the eyes of historians today as Saladin, a noble warrior who displayed mercy for his enemies, is denied the praise and recognition he deserves.

43

KARL MARX

Over the years since its inception Communism has led to the death of millions of people, created the Cold War, the space race and the advancement of atomic weaponry. Incorrectly perceived as a religion, this highly influential economic and political ideology continues to exist today, although increasingly less prominent than the era immediately after its formation by Karl Marx. Born on May 5th, 1818, in Trier, Prussia, modern day Germany, Marx studied law and philosophy, despite descending from generations of rabbis. An early influence on Marx was a philosophy professor, Georg Wilhelm Hegel, who advanced a theory on the evolving process of history whereby harmony can be realized through the equality of opposing factors. Marx originally entertained a career in teaching, yet when his mentor was dismissed due to religious beliefs, Marx turned his attention toward journalism.

While earning a doctorate in philosophy Marx was able to work his way up from a contributing writer to editor of a Prussian periodical, yet the radical political commentary expressed within eventually caused its closure by the Prussian government after less than two years. Marx, now a targeted militant in Prussia, moved to Paris in 1843, continuing to author articles and further his educational development within the ever-growing socialistic community. While in Paris, in 1844, Marx met and developed a friendship with fellow socialist and political activist Friedrich Engels, the man who became the major influence in Marx's life. A lifelong friendship commenced, as well as an effective literary and social partnership that would later change the course of 20th century politics and warfare. Had it not been for the financial assistance provided by Engels to Marx throughout his life, Marx's ideas may never have reached fruition on paper.

Marx traveled extensively in Europe, primarily due to repeated expulsions from countries for contrary political principles. Times were volatile throughout Europe as multiple monarchies were involved in programs of counter-revolution, to control the citizenry and maintain hereditary aristocracy. Marx's concepts were in direct contrast to the goals of these monarchial alliances thus making him a dangerous extremist in certain circles. In 1848, Marx had one of his two most influential treatises published, *The Communist*

Manifesto. Written jointly with Engels, the treatise is an indictment of capitalism, instigating the proletariat to join forces in the battle against neo-feudalism. This major work formed the origin of the communist movement. Viewed as a revolutionary agitator Marx moved to London in 1849, where he would spend the rest of his life in pursuit of acceptance of his political economic theory.

The culmination of over fifteen years of research was realized with the 1867 publication of *Das Kapital*, an argument that economic concepts such as labor theory and surplus value as well as exploitation of the proletariat results in profit decline, which in turn shall inevitably trigger the demise of capitalism. Marx's work included an historical analysis of capitalism in an effort to describe the eventual weaknesses he believed would cause its failure, while offering a structure that was sociological in nature. His research was based entirely on capitalism within his current home, England, which happened to be the most industrialized country of Marx's era. Only the first volume of Marx's work was published in his own lifetime, before he passed away on March 14th, 1883. Later volumes were published posthumously, based on Marx's research and data, yet critiques of these later editions imply a failure to develop a number of Marx's basic principles.

Karl Marx's major contribution to economics and philosophy was creating a scientific approach, much like a biologist or a mathematician, to otherwise previously relegated social and chiefly political sciences. Also a founder president of one of the earliest unions in 1864, Marx strove to unite the world's working classes to achieve increased working conditions. Although no country adopted Marx's principles during his own lifetime, in the early 20th century communism was widely implemented. Also, a number of Marx's economic insights have never come to fruition, most notably the elimination of the middle class. In its basest terms Marx saw economics as the struggles between classes. The infamous tag line regarding Marx's ideology correctly reveals, '*communism works, in theory*'. Regrettably human beings exist in the real world, not in a theoretical environment.

42

LEONARDO DA VINCI

The Renaissance era produced a group of thinkers who excelled at numerous artistic endeavors and scientific enterprises. The period itself became known for such men encompassing the way human potential was viewed as a result of their multiple ventures. No field of study was out of the realm of possibility for these men and the one man who embodied the Renaissance more than any other was Leonardo da Vinci. Born on April 15th, 1452 in the small town of Vinci, located in Tuscany, Italy, Leonardo's father was a notary and his mother was a peasant woman. The couple never married. Leonardo's artistic talent displayed itself at an early age and he was sent to Florence to apprentice with leading Renaissance painter Andrea Verrocchio at the age of 18. Leonardo would go onto become court painter to Lorenzo de Medici, of the ruling Medici family, at the age of 25 outgrowing his master Verrocchio. The most famous work by Leonardo during this time would be uncompleted, titled *The Adoration of the Magi*. Unfortunately this pattern of uncompleted projects would continue throughout his lifetime.

Leonardo left Florence in 1482 to work for the Duke of Milan at which time Leonardo turned his talents to a wide array of topics including anatomy, biology, civil engineering, mathematics, physics and aviation. One of his two most renowned completed paintings, *The Last Supper*, occurred during this time. After leaving Milan in 1499 Leonardo worked for the ruthless military leader Cesare Borgia between 1502 and 1503, who was undertaking a campaign to unite the warring states of Italy under the leadership of the church and employed Leonardo as both a mapmaker and a military engineer. The exile of Borgia to Spain freed up Leonardo to continue his career as an artist and scientist, beginning work on his masterpiece, the *Mona Lisa*. Completed between the end of 1504 and early part of 1505, this painting of a young Tuscan woman has become the most famous painting the world has known. The deep stare of her eyes has been theorized to reveal the author's own depiction of his unparalleled genius. The lack of a smile on the woman's face has been suggested as reflecting Leonardo's own dismay at the death of his father in 1504. Internal expression through painting and other projects allowed Leonardo to deal with his own suffering while not allowing it to affect his genius for thought.

He would now turn his efforts toward the realm of science. Returning to Milan in 1506, Leonardo initiated work in the field of aviation. His scientific contributions in this field include the invention of the helicopter, advancements in the parachute and designs for numerous flying machines emanating from his studies on the flight patterns of birds. Were it not for the lack of a power plant facility his design for the helicopter would have been fully functional and changed the course of history. In 1513 Leonardo traveled to Rome to obtain the patronage of the new Pope Leo X through the Pope's brother Giuliano de' Medici. Leonardo was provided with a workshop to operate on various projects for the Pope, who despite allowing Leonardo the freedom to continue his theoretical research forbade him to perform dissections on cadavers. In 1516 he was offered the position of Premier Painter, Engineer and Architect for the King of France Francis I. He was given a manor house and stipend to allow his full creativity to flow, but soon after he was afflicted with paralysis of the hand. This shortcoming did not negatively affect Leonardo's work as he continued to sketch and paint until his death on May 2nd, 1519.

Other major projects during his period in Milan included engineering work on the Adda River, detailed anatomical research, geological surveys, botanical studies, powerful works of art which remained a lifelong passion, hydraulics and mechanics, blueprints for a submarine, optics and alchemy, deriving from his research on the three primary elements, air, water and fire. Despite the fact that some of these projects went uncompleted Leonardo's detailed notebooks that survived present the insight of an unparalleled genius. His inventive brilliance is neither argued nor dismissed today. Most noted scholars agree that Leonardo Da Vinci was merely born into the world too early, in an era where his mastery and innovative genius could not be fulfilled simply because of the mechanical limitations of the time, limitations that were finally bypassed in large part due to Leonardo's ideas. The zeal for intellectual advancement exhibited by Leonardo in all aspects of his work denotes a truly modern thinker in a time when controversial thought was scorned.

42

41

ERATOSTHENES

The library at Alexandria, Egypt has been theorized as possibly containing all the ancient knowledge in the world that had been translated into written text. Prior to the two fires that may have destroyed valuable information on every field from science to history to religion, those who had complete access to this information were given a true gift and few men in history could have had so much wealth of knowledge under their control and use it to their advantage. Eratosthenes was one of those men. Born in 276 B.C. in Syrene, North Africa, modern day Libya, the bulk of his early years were spent under the tutelage of numerous scholars, philosophers and poets before relocating to Athens to continue his studies. Through tutoring the son of Ptolemy III, Eratosthenes was introduced to the famous library, becoming only the third librarian for the legendary center of knowledge. Described as an all around scholar, he just fell short of the highest rank of expert in any one specific field of knowledge.

With such a wealth of knowledge at his disposal it seems apparent that Eratosthenes delved into a wide array of fields of thought. Such fields included temporal and physical astronomy, mathematics specifically relating to geometry, ethics, world history and geography. Practical mathematics dominated his scholarly work influencing breakthroughs and advancements in all related fields of thought. Within astronomy Eratosthenes developed a map of the solar system that included a catalogue of approximately 675 stars, based primarily on prior deductions and empirical research. He introduced the practice of a calendar made up of 365 days with the addition of one day every fourth year, the 'leap year', which is currently used today. His major breakthrough in the field of astronomy was the almost pinpoint accurate measurement of the circumference of the earth. He also accurately measured the distance from the earth to both the Moon and the Sun based on empirical research of lunar eclipses.

His contributions to other fields include a sieve for prime numbers, which became an essential element in number theory research and a possible mechanical solution for duplicating the cube, long thought to be unsolvable, which was an early precursor to the application of quantum mechanics to the field of mathematics. The field of geography was enhanced by a sketch of the route of the Nile River to explain the flooding in lower tributaries. He also classified the races within the region of Yemen, which added to his scholarly work in the field of cultural and geographical anthropology. In his endeavors of world history Eratosthenes started a project to develop a systematic chronology of major events from the 12th century B.C. to his present time. This helped establish continued historical chronologies of the past and present. His geographical maps and research allowed for the development of civilizations in areas where natural disasters such as flooding could not be fundamentally deciphered, leading toward additional seafaring exploration and discovery.

Eratosthenes' developments in the field of astronomy paved the way for Ptolemy who would become the unquestioned authority for over a millennia. More than simply inspiring others, Eratosthenes measuring the Earth had specific applicable ramifications. By arriving at an almost accurate estimate of the circumference of the Earth implied that Eratosthenes believed the Earth was in fact round, seventeen centuries before Ferdinand Magellan needed to circumnavigate the globe to adjust the accepted opinion regarding the topo-graphy of the earth's surface. While this endeavor cross-references his work in the field of geography, Eratosthenes cultivated his knowledge on a multitude of levels to arrive at theoretical solutions. The work of Eratosthenes has such vital implications that it is difficult to list them all in such a short space.

His time at the library of Alexandria is displayed in the many treatises attributed to him, which are currently lost today, presumably burned in the fire. His method of applying established knowledge to further progress learning and academia set the tone for future advancements in a multitude of fields. At the time of his death in 194 B.C. the library at Alexandria has reached its apex of scholasticism. It can be argued that once Eratosthenes went blind he felt that he could no longer improve upon the knowledge of the world opting instead to end his days by voluntarily starving himself. Without the means to add to human thought, culture and education the legendary all around scholar Eratosthenes simply did not have the desire to continue.

40

JOHN STUART MILL

Victorian England was an austere era of demanding values placed upon the individual. The periods own rigidity often hampered its social advancement in favor of uniformity and compliance to societal morays. A free thinker would suffocate in such and environment, or conversely battle to change the accepted systems of thought. John Stuart Mill chose the latter, perhaps due to his upbringing, within a strict regimented educational environment. Mill is often described as having been neglected a childhood in favor of an entire adulthood. Born in London on May 20th, 1806, Mill was reading Greek at three and Latin soon thereafter. His studies, conducted solely by his father, included logic, philosophy, mathematics, law and of course languages, completing what amounted to an entire university education by fourteen. Due to his advanced scholastic aptitude Mill would contribute articles to a utilitarian journal while still a teenager. His aptitude and literary skill displayed itself at such an early age that it seems almost criminal that writing remained a hobby rather than a profession.

In 1823 Mill joined his father in working for the East India Company, where he would remain until the firm dissolved in 1858. After his father's mental breakdown Mill moved away from the pure utilitarian beliefs of his father, not thoroughly disengaging himself from utilitarianism, yet rather evolving a radical new approach, which included aspects of both positivism and humanism. These ideological variations would become a recurring factor in Mill's later writings on a wide range of social subjects. Among Mill's most significant treatises are; *A System of Logic* in 1843, *Principles of Political Economy*, in 1848, *On Liberty*, in 1859 and *The Subjection of Women* in 1869, the latter having been influenced by his recently departed wife, a feminist in her own right. Between 1865 and 1868 Mill served as the Parliamentary representative for Westminster. During his short tenure in Parliament Mill actively fought to reduce the national debt and was a diligent advocate for women's suffrage. Mill would retire to Avignon, France where he would pass away on May 7th, 1873.

The first two paramount works of Mill's are his dissertations on logic and political economy. The 1843 work was based on the theories of scientist

Isaac Newton whereby Mill endeavored to devise a logical approach to social sciences based on empirical research. In attempting to systematically justify the value and necessity of social sciences, Mill began a mission that has still yet to be accomplished. An effort to enhance the validity of the social sciences continues to be undertaken yet a major pioneer in this enterprise was Mill. Mill's 1848 work on political economy became the leading economic textbook in the field for more than fifty years after its publication. His 1869 work became the classic statement for the women's suffrage movement. Continuing along his humanistic tone Mill discussed the lack of education, Victorian ethics and negative status of women throughout history. While women were attempting to gain equality as far back as 1789 in France and 1792 in England, their cries often fell upon deaf ears. Mill's work toward equality of the sexes spearheaded the advancement of the women's suffrage movement by installing a well-respected male figure as a prime activist. No longer could the world turn a blind eye.

Mill's 1859 work is perhaps his most critically acclaimed and the one for which he is most remembered. *On Liberty* is perhaps the greatest social commentary on individual rights versus the rights of the state. The work was a major thesis on political liberalism where a *laissez-faire* attitude is encouraged regarding an individual's choices so long as those choices do not adversely affect others. A theoretical basis for democratic ethics and morality, the thesis' defense of the rights of individual freedom cements its status as one of the leading philosophical arguments against governmental control. The philosophical, economic and social effects that Mill has offered society have evolved the ideals of humanity. As trivial as these principles appear today, they were revolutionary to the Victorian world, which embraced these landmark innovations originated by Mill. His work creates the foundation for evolving social philosophy and the emergence of political correctness. His father's determination on educating his son to the utmost developed one of the purest thinkers of the modern age. John Stuart Mill, more than anything, was a pioneer in the advancement of unpopular thought, just so long as it improved society. The betterment of society was Mill's ultimate goal.

50

39

KONG QIU ZHONGNI (KUNG FU-TZU)

Prior to the 6th century B.C. China was a mixture of several religious philosophies that promoted discord throughout separate regions. These differences in spiritual thought often led to war between provinces. While war would remain a constant, a harmonization of beliefs systems was needed to promote unity within China. This personally meaningful project was undertaken by Kong Qiu Zhongni, known to the West by his Latinized name Confucius. Widely considered as one of the most renowned and influential philosophers that has ever lived, Confucius was born in 551 B.C., in the state of Lu, in Northeast China. His father passed away when he was only three, leaving him to be raised by his mother in poverty. During his adolescence Confucius became the family provider, employed in a number of different menial jobs, although a love of learning was readily apparent throughout his youth. Married at the age of nineteen, but divorced four years later, Confucius would also have to deal with the death of his mother shortly thereafter. Confucius' love and reverence for the past exhibited itself during his mother's burial ceremony and the following three years of mourning. Afterwards, he devoted his time to the study of philosophy, exploring and embracing archaic values that would later translate into core principles within his philosophical approach to life.

Confucius embarked on a career in civil service, yet his early attempts as a politician were a distinct failure. Various attempts to push for the implementation of his own belief system failed and Confucius eventually left his post around the age of 35, forced into exile by the new ruling family. He traveled from state to state, performing a dualistic role of philosopher / politician, attempting to apply his basic principles to create a perfect society. These principles included the citizenry retaining a designated role and upholding that responsibility, and government displaying their generosity to the people by promoting morality, education and a quality standard of living. These policies were difficult to adopt in ancient times as states waged battles for supremacy, so Confucius returned to Lu and was granted a relatively high-ranking position in the government, perhaps as a result of his storied reputation. Four years later he was exiled again from Lu due to political enemies at court, which allowed him to continue his travels, spreading the nature of his ideas from state to state. He would once again return to Lu in 484 B.C., never to leave his home again.

Confucianism, to start off with, is not a religion. That is a fundamental inaccuracy often made by historians who measure the widespread acceptance of the Confucian ideal system throughout China over the span of more than two thousand years rather than its actual philosophy. Confucianism is a set of moral and ethical beliefs, to properly guide men in a search for harmony between each other within society, as opposed to a preparatory spiritual accord for the afterlife. This critical distinction differentiates Confucianism from standard religious doctrine into the realm of philosophy. Two essential values within the Confucian belief system are the *jen* and the *li*, roughly translated as compassionate concern for others and proper conduct, respectively. Confucius believed that possession of these two values were imperative to the *chun-tzu*, the superior man. An imperative aspect of Confucian teaching was based on the *I Ching*, where moderation and temperance were keys to maintaining balance within oneself.

The Confucian ideal was adopted by China as the nationalistic viewpoint shortly after his death in 479 B.C. Successive scholars within the Chou dynasty were taught in the Confucian system, and in turn trained the youth in these ideals. During the short-lived reign of the Ch'in dynasty, Confucianism was abolished, as the teachings of Confucianism were censored and practicing scholars executed, yet would be reinstated and remain the national philosophy until 1911. The most honored ideal to Confucius was filial piety, an adoration of elders, a sense that developed early in life and has resulted in a time honored tradition in Chinese culture withstanding the test of time and an ever-changing world. Confucius also established a school, open to whoever was willing to listen, where he was able to teach his values on the importance of education in the development of the individual. As a result Confucius was able to spread his message throughout the land, which later in life helped establish his reputation as a sage among men. His love of purity and harmony through inner peace allowed a rural country to avoid destroying itself from within while his teachings continue to offer valuable life lessons regarding the co-existence of human beings within society.

54

38

FLAVIUS ANICIUS PETRUS SABBATIUS JUSTINIANUS

The once mighty Roman Empire had fell on hard times with the fall of the Western half in 476 A.D. The numerous barbarian hordes had crippled what was once the most magnificent empire in Western civilization. The Eastern half of the Roman Empire felt the strain of changing times as Europe headed toward the Dark Ages, but one man fought hard to return his empire to glory and under Emporer Justinian I, the Roman Empire had briefly regained its status as the most powerful dynasty in Europe. Born under the name Uprauda around May 11th, 483 A.D. in Tauresium, present day Yugoslavia, Flavius rose to the title of Justinian I, Holy Roman Emporer in the East. Extremely little is known of the early part of Justinian's life. His ancestry was Barbaian, either Teutonic or Slavonic. He studied at Constantinople while a young man, obtaining a varied education in language, philosophy and law, the latter displayed by many of his later reforms. Flavius took a Roman name from his uncle Justin, chief of the Imperial guard who later ascended to the throne as Emporer in 518. The throne however, was run by Justinian, who would be eventually crowned Emperor in 527.

The first year after rising to Emporer, Justinian began his most renowned accomplishment, the codification of law within the Roman Empire in the East. A commission was organized with the specific task of creating a structured system of Imperial laws and only one year later, in 529, the first draft of these laws was made public, although the *Corpus Juris Civilis*, as it was called, was not ratified until 534. The code of laws systematized an amalgam of newly created decrees and elder policies that remained important and essential. All other previous laws and edicts were annulled. Also in 529 Justinian closed the almost 1,000 year-old Academy of Philosophy in Athens founded by Plato. Justinian's closure of the academy was a response to paganism, which he felt was taught and promulgated by professors, rather than an attack on western philosophy. Later Justinian condemned the writings of Origen, an important 3rd century theologian, labeling him as a heretic. These two direct attacks on ancient Greek scholarship evolved out of Justinian's desire to stabilize the Roman Empire and return it to the glory it had seen in past days.

The many facets to Justinian's rule as Emperor included regaining the territories from the Western part of the Roman Empire, lost since the time of Emperor Constantine in the early 4th century. A succession of invaders conquered Roman lands and Justinian saw it as a personal battle to restore supremacy by re-conquering these lands. Under the leadership of his General, Belisarius, a series of battles were waged. Justinian and Belisarius defended the Empire in the east by thwarting all Persian attacks, and later conquered Carthage from the Vandals. In 535 Belisarius attacked the Ostrogoths and reclaimed Sicily, Naples, Rome and finally Milan and Ravenna, the Ostrogoth capital in 540. In 550 a civil war between the Visigoths in Spain allowed Justinian to reclaim the long lost southern Roman provinces taken by the Visigoths. He was slowly succeeding in restoring the empire.

In November of 565 Justinian would pass away, succeeded by his nephew Justin II. Justinian's numerous conquests allowed for the expansion of Christianity during the Middle and Dark ages and the virtual eradication of the Vandals, a barbarian tribe of Germanic descent. Byzantium was never conquered, remaining a Christian held municipality until 1453. When Justinian took over the throne, the empire was in legal disarray. Justinian's codices of law helped strengthen the internal power of the Roman Empire, which in turn allowed the military expansion of those previously lost areas, once held under Roman rule. During the latter part of the Middle Ages Justinian's laws became the benchmark of the European legal system and even countries outside of Europe adopted elements of the Justinian code as they applied to civil regulations.

While Justinian is primarily associated with the above codification of Roman laws, the closure of Plato's Academy in Athens has the deepest ramifications. Western philosophy and thought under the guise of stamping out Hellenism was dealt a serious blow. This move may have directly led to the inception of the Dark ages within Europe, whereby the seat of Western philosophy relocated to the Arabian Peninsula, creating a mecca for thought and scientific discovery. During the 10th through the 12th centuries Islamic scholars revived Western philosophy in Europe thus completing the unnecessary circle instituted by Justinian in 529 to save his own empire. Both positive and negative, Justinian's modifications greatly affected the world for generations.

37

SIDDHARTHA GAUTAMA

Throughout history man's search for internal peace has led toward the evolvement of numerous ideas and philosophies, among them the search for spiritual harmony. While exploring the nature of one's self often times an inevitable turn toward religion and an internal investigation of man's true purpose commences. The founder of one of these quests, and one of the world's oldest and most followed religions, was a Nepalese Prince, Siddhartha Gautama. Born in 563 B.C, in Lumbina, present day Nepal, his father however, King Suddhodana, ruled over a small region that lay within India. Siddhartha led the life of nobility, never wanting for anything, sheltered from the outside world for the entirety of his early days. At the age of sixteen he was wed to a princess from a neighboring region, believed to have been his cousin. During his days at the palace Siddhartha studied philosophy and Hindu literature to gain a better understanding of the world. Up until the age of twenty-nine Siddhartha had only ventured outside the shielded walls of the palace on four occasions, each time encountering a man in a different state of life, later to be known in Buddhism as the Four Meetings. While specifics are unclear regarding these meetings they completely impacted a sheltered man who had become disenchanted with the banality of nobility. After the birth of his first child a discontented Siddhartha decided to search the outside world for spiritual enlightenment.

Siddhartha practiced a variety of religions in his effort to understand the necessity for human suffering and pain, seeking out the wisdom of numerous holy men, who practiced a pseudo religion known as asceticism. While the practices of these holy men could not satisfy his thirst for an answer, Siddhartha believed in their specific ideas, and as a result, sought out a specific religious sect of asceticism known as Jainism. Jainism taught the immortality of the soul while denying the existence of a supreme being. Siddhartha practiced Jainism for a number of years, engaging in fasts of an extreme nature in an attempt to overcome bodily desires, taking asceticism to a higher spiritual level. This self-enforced torture of the body and mind provided no answer to Siddhartha, who abandoned asceticism altogether and observed a life of solitude. At the age of thirty-five, after spending a night meditating under a giant fig tree, Siddhartha believed he had finally attained a spiritual awakening. Immediately Siddhartha journeyed throughout the region preaching his newfound understanding, gathering followers wherever he traveled. He became known as the Buddha, or enlightened one.

The main teachings of Siddhartha included principles known as the Four Noble Truths. First, all existence is suffering and there is no escape from the pain of existence. Second, the cause of this suffering arises out of desire. Third, a release from suffering occurs when desire ceases to exist, and fourth, the way to end suffering is through a course of action known as the Eight-Fold Path. This path includes right views, right thought, right speech, right action, right livelihood, right effort, right mindfulness and right meditation. Through following the Eight-Fold Path one can accomplish a spiritual state of peace known as *nirvana*. The achieving of this was the ultimate goal of any righteous person. For the final forty-five years of his life Siddhartha taught the basic principles of Buddhism, eventually passing away in 483 B.C. Siddhartha never wrote down any of his teachings on paper, yet the numerous followers he gathered continued his teaching relying on oral tradition. It would not be until centuries after his death when his practices were properly recorded, although by this time Buddhism has split into two alternate branches. Due to the conversion of the 3rd century B.C. Indian Emperor Asoka, Buddhism began to obtain a larger following, branching out into other countries, eventually making its way into Tibet and Japan, where it remains as a dominant religion critical to daily life.

In establishing a major world religion, Siddhartha Gautama altered the course of Asian history, equally preventing and unconsciously creating conflict and debate that continues today. Buddhism offered a spiritual outlet for those Northern Indians who were precluded from the practicing the national religion of Hinduism based on the caste system, while at the same time proposing an alternative solution to ending intrinsic suffering. Siddhartha's vision of an ideal path toward enlightenment, achieved through spiritual empiricism, allowed previously fixed tradition to be altered and adapted to one's experimental spiritual journeys. This freedom extended itself into other areas of life, where freedom of thought, in a rigid environment, could now be widely accepted.

62

36

ADOLF HITLER

In the second quarter of the 20th century the world faced a very serious threat, the rise of a ruthless political system marked by centralized control under a dictator and control of opposing ideas through terrorism and extreme racism. Known as Fascism, those who practiced this ideology attempted a large-scale takeover, starting within Eastern Europe while organizing plans for ruling the world and eradicating all who opposed. While not the originator of the fascist ideals, its most notable public figure, considered by many to be the most evil man who ever lived, was Adolf Hitler. Born on April 20th, 1889, in the small town of Braunau-am-Inn, Austria, his early education was not filled with accolades, yet Hitler developed a talent for painting. Unfortunately he was rejected by the Vienna Academy of Fine Arts. Hitler worked odd jobs until leaving for Germany to escape serving in the Austrian armed forces, but would later join the German military, involved in World War I.

Hitler, a corporal, was wounded twice, the final injury occurring only four weeks prior to the end of the war. By the time Hitler had recuperated, World War I had ended in defeat for Germany, and he began his political indoctrination. Initially acting as a spy, Hitler was sent to monitor a small group known as the German Workers' Party. By September of 1919 Hitler had become a member of this party, acknowledging a similarity in principles. Less than a year later the party was renamed the National Socialist German Workers' Party; Nazi for short. Hitler would be recognized as the party's leader. With the Nazi Party growing stronger, mainly due to the powerful and highly influencing oratory skills possessed by Hitler, a military style engagement was inevitable.

In late 1923 the Hitler led Nazi Party attempted a coup d'etat of the Bavarian government in Munich. The coup failed and Hitler was arrested, tried and sentenced to five years imprisonment. Hitler would only serve nine months of his sentence, yet he would dictate what he considered to be his masterpiece, *Mein Kampf*, a Social Darwinist approach outlining the superiority of the Aryan race. Considered today to be extreme Fascist propaganda Hitler's autobiography spoke to a nation in disarray, which Hitler cunningly was able to use to his advantage. A fine-tuning of the Nazi Party's agenda occurred over the next couple of years with their following considerably increasing in political circles.

Hitler was appointed Chancellor of Germany on January 30th, 1933, and the following year Hitler assumed full control and embarked upon a path that led toward World War II.

By establishing a Fascist state in Germany, Hitler immediately broke the conditions of the Treaty of Versailles by re-arming the military. Unions were formed with Italy and Japan, and had it not been for an Allied victory in World War II Hitler would have outgrown the necessity of keeping such a coalition, as he felt they too were beneath the Aryan German. In addition to Hitler's military endeavors an overlooked consequence directly attributable to Adolf Hitler is the advancement of nuclear weaponry. German physicists were instructed to develop atomic weapons for purposes of mass destruction. As a result the United States, among other countries, became insistent on developing nuclear weaponry for aggression and ultimately protection. These amazing discoveries advanced the field of nuclear physics, opening up the possibility for further developments in military weaponry, including chemical and biological devices for aggressive military purposes. Hitler's vision, as one-sided as it was, paved the way for future developments in military warfare.

Adolf Hitler was an evil man. There is no denying that simple fact. Understanding him is an expedition into megalomania. Hitler was a product of not only his time, but also an environment ripe for a leader who embodied a spirit that would bring about a radical change. Hitler's oratory capacity for reaching the hearts and minds of a community in need, reeling from the after effects of War and upcoming economic struggles, aided the re-birth and development of anti-Semitic hatred. Such hatred almost eliminated opposing thought and ideas that would have returned man to an evolutionary stone age. Without the leadership of Adolf Hitler the Nazi party and German Fascism disintegrated, setting the stage for communism and the Cold War. Hitler's legacy of hatred unfortunately still remains throughout the world today, in the form of racial and cultural oppression and global terrorism. As defeat approached Germany in World War II, Hitler committed suicide, in an underground bunker where he had been hiding; cowardly avoiding the chaos he helped create.

35

IGNAC FULOP SEMMELWEIS

The solution to halting the spread of harmful bacteria and disease has baffled the medical community since the dawn of medicine. Advancing technologies within medicine, including a greater knowledge of anatomy and physiology, the role of chemistry in medicine, increased quantity and quality of medical facilities and overall awareness in all medical related fields did not seem to prevent the problem of contagious bacteria. It was in the eighteenth century when the first epidemics of puerperal fever, also known as childbed fever, arose. In 1847, a Hungarian named Semmelweis began to make the first major strides by analyzing and interpreting the epidemic of puerperal fever.

Born on July 1st, 1818 in a small center of Buda, Hungary, Semmelweis was the fifth child of a middle-class shopkeeper. His early schooling took place at the Catholic Gymnasium in Buda, eventually moving onto the University of Pest, graduating in 1837, and then leaving for Vienna, Austria and a career in law and bureaucracy. Once in Vienna, Semmelweis had a career change, enrolling in the Viennese medical school, returning after only one year's work to complete his medical studies at the University of Pest. In 1841 Semmelweis returned to Vienna, enrolling at the Second Vienna Medical School. Semmelweis graduated in 1844, although he decided to remain in Vienna to complete surgical training. Starting out as an assistant in the University of Vienna's teaching hospital, Semmelweis went on to become the house officer for the First Obstetrical Clinic in July of 1846. It was in this position where he began to notice the abhorrent mortality rates as a result of puerperal fever, and also that they were rising.

In 1846 there were two clinics dedicated to obstetrics at the University of Vienna's teaching hospital. Semmelweis noticed the extreme difference in mortality rates from puerperal fever. The First Obstetrical Clinic had a mortality rate of over 13%, almost double that of the previous year, while the Second Clinic's mortality rate was just barely above 2%. Semmelweis viewed the extreme difference in the mortality rate of the First Clinic from the Second Clinic as perhaps the key to eradicating the epidemic. The First Clinic was designed for the teaching of medical students, while the Second Clinic was solely intended for the instruction of midwives. The difference between these two clinics was that the medical students were moving from the autopsy rooms to the maternity wards without washing their hands. The death of a friend would confirm this.

In 1847 Semmelweis' friend Jakob Kolletschka died from an infection after sustaining a knife puncture during a post-mortem examination. The autopsy displayed symptoms similar to puerperal fever as the cause of death. Semmelweis immediately made the connection. He began insisting that all medical personnel wash and sterilize their hands when working with cadavers, then patients. Immediately the mortality rate from puerperal fever dropped to under 3%, almost as low as the Second Clinic. Without revealing his results Semmelweis continued with his thorough efforts by enforcing the sterilization of all medical instruments designed for labor. This second step effectively eliminated puerperal fever. This concept led to the creation of the germ theory of disease and the implementation of antiseptic measures during surgery. Through his pioneering achievements in medicine, Semmelweis eventually helped to save millions and perhaps billions of future lives.

The medical establishment rejected Semmelweis' finding for two baseless reasons, firstly they were made during the European revolutionary year of 1848 when men in power were forced to choose sides in political battles rather than endorse innovative changes, and secondly doctors were unwilling to admit they were somehow responsible for extremely high mortality rates. The old medical establishment still believed death was caused by medical imbalances within the human body. Semmelweis left Vienna and continued his sterilization practices in his native Hungary, where he continued to eradicate deaths resulting from puerperal fever. In 1861 he published his findings, yet received critical condemnation. Ignac Semmelweis passed away in 1865 from blood poisoning, while confined within an insane asylum. He would never see his brilliant vision come to fruition, and the effect it would have upon the lives of future generations. Semmelweis is considered to be medicine's greatest unrecognized hero, arising from his passion for the preservation of human life above standard medical practices. The fight of medical revolutionaries like Semmelweis continues today.

34

ODO DE LAGERY

In the 9th century A.D. the Catholic Church began to assert their political power by aligning themselves with strong European monarchies to gain a spiritual foothold within Europe, similar to the one the Roman Empire had ruled hundreds of years previously. After the death of Charlemagne, Europe was in disarray with countries waging continuous warfare against one another primarily over territorial disputes. Despite the prominence and ascendancy of the Catholic Church during this period in history their attempts at unifying Western Christianity had failed, until a single speech was given by Odo De Lagery. The Crusades, considered the bloodiest wars in recorded history, can be traced back to this speech, on November 27th, 1095, on a platform at Clermont, France. Alternate dates of Odo's birth are 1035 or 1042, in Chatillon-sur-Marne, France. His family was of French nobility and knighthood, extremely religious, and Odo would enter a life of religious servitude, first becoming an archdeacon before becoming a monk, studying under the renowned abbot St. Hugh. Odo would move to Rome and be appointed Cardinal-Bishop in 1078. Odo served Pope Gregory VII in Germany from 1082 to 1085, focusing on reform from prior church abuses. Odo was elected Pope on March 12th, 1088, taking the name Urban II. His reign as Pope would be a tumultuous one.

Odo's main goal was reform and he preached to the territories that recognized his papal authority. Then there was the November 27th, 1095 speech. This speech arose out of a plea for assistance from Byzantine Emporer Alexius II against the marauding Seljuk Turks. Odo seized this as an opportunity to unite the battling armies of Western Christianity to regain Jerusalem, considered as rightfully belonging to Christendom. As the Christian Crusaders made their way toward regaining Jerusalem, their raiding became that of legend. All that stood in their way was destroyed and those opposing them were murdered, including some of those they were intending to help. Odo had manipulated the Crusaders by promising untold riches and salvation from their sins. Their overzealous behavior was viewed as forgiven for accomplishing the work of God. In this, an absolute disregard for clemency and mankind, despite differences in religious beliefs, was employed, primarily out of a papal approval of salvation for services rendered. When the Christian Crusaders reclaimed Jerusalem in 1099, the news did not reach Odo before his death on July 29th, two weeks after his Crusade succeeded. He would also not bear witness to the seven Crusades that followed over almost two hundred years, and the senseless bloodshed that were their aftermath.

The Crusades that took place after the original 1095 Crusade should not be attributed to Pope Urban II, although they easily could be. It cannot be denied that the original Crusade would never have taken place without the initiative of Odo. Christians or not, if anyone other than a papal leader had called upon Christendom to reclaim the Holy land the original Crusade would have failed, as Christians from different kingdoms and provinces were constantly battling each other over their own territories. United under a religious leader such as the Pope Urban II, this ensured that the first Crusade would succeed. The later Crusades were obviously sparked by the first Crusade and the speech at Clermont in 1095. Their failures to reclaim Jerusalem only reassures that the key figure with regards to the Christian Crusades was Odo de Lagery, Pope Urban II.

The Christian Crusades are perhaps one of the most significant events in European history. The infusion of Islamic and Eastern culture into Western Europe denotes the Crusades as an episode that single handedly changed the face of Europe. As a result, Europe was ultimately led out of the Middle Ages into a scientific revolution. One particular item from the East, papermaking, altered the course of Western history. Europe was considerably less advanced than the Far and Middle East, yet as a result of the Crusades and an introduction into Eastern culture, Europe was able to make momentous advancements in both culture and science, inevitably allowing them to progress ahead of the Eastern world and pave the way toward an era of enlightenment and discovery. Odo De Lagery's religious zeal was viewed throughout the realm of Christianity as divinely inspired. The unification of the Eastern and Western Empires of Christianity was perhaps the only positive result of the Crusades, for which he was later beatified in 1881. His many positive reform movements continued through the work of successive Popes, yet unfortunately the carnage and aftermath of the bloody wars he initiated will be the main basis for his lasting legacy throughout history.

74

33

ELIZABETH TUDOR

Resulting from external wars with France and internal wars over succession to the throne during the 13th and 14th centuries England had become a land in disarray. Further turmoil continued in the 16th century as religion and infidelity played a pivotal role in fracturing a nation. England was in dire need of a representative to lift their spirits and ascend them to glory, yet no one could have predicted England's savior would come in the form of a 25 year-old woman. Elizabeth was born on September 7th, 1533 in Greenwich, England to King Henry VIII and his second wife Anne Boleyn, yet at the age of three Elizabeth was declared illegitimate by Parliament after her mother was beheaded. The death of Henry VIII in 1547 left the throne to his only male heir, Edward VI who died in 1553 and the throne was then handed to Henry VIII's daughter, Mary I, a devout Roman Catholic who used her short reign to promote religious persecution. In 1558, after surviving imprisonment in the Tower of London, Elizabeth I took her rightful place as Queen. It is commonly acknowledged that the forty-five year reign of Elizabeth I is considered the Golden Age of England.

When Elizabeth's reign began England was in the midst of economic distress and religious upheaval that had England on the brink of War. Elizabeth immediately took steps to satisfy the ongoing religious issues by establishing Anglican as the official religion of England. Mary Stuart, Queen of Scotland, was Elizabeth's main political rival. She was an ardent Catholic involved in numerous plots to overthrow Elizabeth. When Mary fled Scotland for England Elizabeth had her imprisoned in 1568, eventually signing her death warrant in 1587. This would not end the fighting and was a partial reason for the attempted invasion by the Spanish Armada in 1588.

England was in a state of economic distress; that is until Elizabeth financed the naval voyages of Francis Drake. Drake was to sail to the Americas to establish trade and capitalize on the lucrative empire that Spain had set up with the New World. Drake's covert plan under Elizabeth was to raid Spanish settlements and ships of their gold and silver for Queen and country. When King Philip II of Spain attempted to invade England it was Drake, under the sponsor-ship of Elizabeth, who handily defeated the much larger Spanish Armada.

Francis Drake's role in English history had a three-fold effect; it opened up the door to English settlements in North America from the prosperity of trade, it recouped the fledgling economy that had been handed to Elizabeth upon ascending to the throne and it thoroughly established England as a naval power. Drake's role, however, would not have existed without the patronage of Queen Elizabeth.

Commencing concurrently with Drake's rise to naval supremacy was Elizabeth's patronage of Walter Raleigh. Due to Raleigh's success in suppressing an Irish rebellion, Elizabeth funded Raleigh's attempts to colonize America, and in 1587 the first English settlement was established. Raleigh returned to England with two important items for trade, the potato and tobacco. The consequences of these two important cash crops led in part to the eventual English colonization of America. Again, while Raleigh significantly helped to initiate future English settlement it was under the impetus of Elizabeth, without whose benefaction, these English settlements may never have led to English colonization in America. At home, the birth of significant English literature occurred, prospering under the creative encouragement of Elizabeth. It is difficult to assess the pivotal function Elizabeth played in the literary advancements during her reign. It is noteworthy that without the subsidies provided by Elizabeth to the arts, this era of English literature might never have flourished, including the works of William Shakespeare, principally considered the most important writer of all time, whose genius was revealed through Elizabeth's patronage.

Economic growth, religious toleration, the inauguration of American colonization, naval ascendancy and literary advancement occurred during her reign, all with her sponsorship. Queen Elizabeth I single handedly changed the future course of her country over a minimal forty-five year period, in effect changing the course of modern world history. Passing away on March 24th, 1603 without an heir, Elizabeth named James VI of Scotland as her successor, whose rigidity, along with his son Charles I, led to the English Civil War. Even after her death the impact of Elizabeth's decisions regarding her country influenced the course of European history.

32

THOMAS MALTHUS

Advances in medicine and industrialization of society created a better and longer life for human beings. Increased health and wealth correlated to an increase in population. Resulting from an ongoing debate between father and son an anonymous essay was published in 1798, developing an age-old principle in such a clear concise manner that it could not be ignored any longer; the imminent problem of overpopulation. Its author, Thomas Malthus, who would influence and shape economic thought values, was born in Surrey, England in 1766. Malthus received his education from private tutors and his father, before entering Jesus College, Cambridge University, graduating in 1788. He earned his Masters Degree three years later and in 1793 was elected a Fellow of Jesus College.

Five years later, while ordained as an Anglican clergyman, Malthus produced the work that would secure his importance in a diverse number of fields. Between 1803 and 1826 Malthus advanced and furthered his own principal thesis on population growth. In 1805 Malthus was appointed Professor of Political Economy, the first known economic position in academia. Offshoots of Malthus' work included the 1815 works on the differential theory of rent and the importation of corn, a debate that was raging in Parliament. His 1820 work *Principles of Political Economy* introduced the modern idea of a demand schedule, an important element in the conceptual theory of supply and demand, contrary however, to the classical economic views of the time.

The 1798 essay and the revisions that followed are the works that Malthus will be most remembered for. Its basic tenets are that while population grows at an exponential rate provisional quantity increases arithmetically, thus indicating that people will eventually outgrow food supply. Malthus' mathematical formula discussing the impending dangers of overpopulation forced the world to take notice. Malthus stated that horrors such as starvation and disease were divine necessities, yet the tendencies of the population to multiply will always outweigh any advances in agriculture. This principle actually presents an anti-Utopian society, which requires an entire shift in values along class lines to resolve the dilemma. This predicament is perfectly displayed in the Poor Laws initiated in England, which produce an adverse effect in that the relief provided increased poverty, as that relief had been utilized unfavorably, producing an added increase in population.

The implications of Malthus' arguments led to the initiation of the census program in 1801, as the population versus agricultural supply needed to be governmentally monitored. An additional implication of Malthus' arguments was the advent of contraceptive measures to limit population. Malthus was not an advocate of the use of contraception, yet it should not be argued that Malthus' essay did not amplify the necessity for the introduction of contraceptive methods into an ever-growing society. The multiplicity of birth control methods that have developed since their initiation into society is a direct result of Malthus' economically structured theory, and adherents to contraceptive measures in checking population are generally termed as neo-Malthusians.

Despite the 1798 essay establishing Malthus as an intellectual giant the general influence his theory had upon later intellects is staggering. English economist David Ricardo based his famous *'Iron Law of Wages'* upon Malthus' hypotheses. Working from Ricardo's principle Karl Marx's theory of surplus value was strongly influenced by aspects of Malthus' class struggle. In 1838 a young biologist named Charles Darwin read Malthus' essay and was able to construct his renowned theory of Natural Selection. Alfred Russell Wallace, Darwin's contemporary, called upon the work of Malthus to arrive at similar conclusions, showing that the work of Thomas Malthus has influenced not only economic theory, yet also has inspired major advances in evolutionary biology. Malthus passed away in 1834 before the inception of Malthusian leagues, devoted to controlling the problem of overpopulation, first created in the 1860's. Where Malthus achieved his legendary stature was through the ability to ignore an early political correctness in favor of scientific theory. Malthus received harsh criticism for his formation of moral restraint, while preaching the divinity of compulsory distress, yet the assumptive certainties of his theory ensured that the predicament of overpopulation would not be disregarded.

31

SHARRU-KIN

Prior to the middle of the 3rd millennia B.C. invading countries allowed the defeated territories to continue to hold ruling power, only enforcing payment to those conquering nations. This did not significantly allow for the true expansion of empires, until one man, Sharru-Kin united an entire group of tribes and established an Imperial framework for expansion and advancement. Known to the world today as Sargon the Great, creator of one of the first recorded dynasties in history, the exact date of Sargon's birth is uncertain, approximated at around the late 24th century B.C. The story of his birth is that of legend, depicted as an illegitimate child to a gardener and a changeling, a priestess and or prostitute of Kish, an ancient city of Mesopotamia. Due to the illegitimacy Sargon was placed in a basket of reeds and set in the Euphrates River. The parallels to the story of the Hebrew prophet Moses are apparent yet outdate the origin of the birth and discovery of Moses by over 1,000 years, while also occurring in a nearby region where legend traveled through oral tradition.

Sargon was rescued and brought up in the court of Ur-Zababa, King of Kish, ultimately occupying the role of cupbearer. Legend has it that Sargon revealed a dream to the King predicting his demise, whereupon Sargon was set up to be murdered by the King of Uruk. Internal errors with this legend are numerous including the two primary facts; envelopes had not yet been invented, which was supposed to contain the hidden document and the two kings involved in the secret assassination plot, were rulers from different generations, who according to recorded history could not have come in contact with each other. What is known to be accurate regarding Sargon is that he left Kish after it was conquered by Lugal-zage-si. He established the beginnings of his empire in the Northern Mesopotamian region of Akkad and the Southern Mesopotamian region of Sumer. Sargon is credited as the first King of the Akkadian dynasty, a Semitic people whose base is in Akkad. Their language is considered to be the oldest Semitic language, and as such, credit must be bestowed upon Sargon for establishing a civilized and culturally expanding empire that allowed the combining of various tribes into one cohesive community.

Once Sargon's forces had become strong enough he began to unite all of the Mesopotamia cities encompassing the Tigris and Euphrates Rivers, extending to parts of Assyria where he is listed as a King and founder of a dynasty in the historical records. The current topography has Sargon's empire reaching from the Persian Gulf to the Mediterranean Sea. Trade, culture and governmental bureaucracy flourished during the fifty-six year reign of Sargon the Great, until it was ended in approximately 2271 B.C. while defending his empire from a revolt. Sargon had two sons, Rimush and Manishtushu, who ascended the throne after his death as per Sargon's design. His sons further extended the empire created by Sargon, and his grandson Narmsin continued along these lines. This was extremely important as a line of hereditary succession was established, which would serve as the model for European monarchies and Asian dynasties to follow. This line of succession was continued until 2219 B.C. when the Guitans, a nomadic people from the Zygros Mountains in Western Iran, conquered Akkad.

Sargon's legend remains as the founder and creator of the Akkadian dynasty. More central to Sargon's rule is that he is the creator and founder of Imperialism. Sargon revolutionized the long-standing practice of a King or General conquering a land yet leaving that land to be run by the conquered empire-towns, with only a stipend or tribute to be paid to the conquering country. In effect, the conquering empire would not adopt the overthrown town into their empire, settling for the specific tribute. Sargon attacked and conquered an empire or region, placing one of his subordinate governors in control of this land to ensure loyalty, prevent major revolts and administer governmental affairs on the recently acquired lands. This supported the entirety of the empire allowing for the possibility of further expansion, the birth of Imperialism. Imperialism prospered during the times of Babylonian, Sumerian and Persian Empires, early Greek city-states, the Roman Empire, the Huns and other Barbarian hordes, the Mongols and continued into the 20th century. Due to the innovations and progress carried out by Sargon the Great historians can establish a distinct line between history and pre-history further advancing our under-standing of the activities of the past.

30

PLATO

Political philosophy has been around for more than two millennia, tracing its roots to ancient Greece. Like all forms of expression political thought has evolved over the course of its history, with underlying factors such as dictatorial monarchies shaping how free thinkers viewed tyranny and oppression. Free thinkers shape the minds of future generations and the originator of the concept of political commentary was the noted philosopher Plato, ensuring that opposing thought, even against reigning authority, was established. Plato was born in approximately 427 B.C. to wealthy and influential parents within Athenian society. Plato grew up during the Peloponnesian War and enlisted to fight for Athens as soon as he was able to. Plato returned to Athens in 408, despite the War not officially ending until 404, to study philosophy under Socrates. Plato considered Socrates the wisest man he had ever met, so when he was arrested for corrupting the minds of the youth of Athens and committed suicide, Plato left Athens, clearly disillusioned with Athenian autocracy for their condemnation of his mentor.

While away from Athens Plato traveled extensively, visiting Egypt, the Middle East, Italy, Greece and the island of Sicily. He acted as a court philosopher during time spent in Sicily, all the while managing to keep clear of politics. Eventually Plato would return to Athens in 387 B.C. where he founded a school, called the Academy, devoted to the advancement of learning and philosophy. The students at the Academy were educated in the Socratic method toward the attainment of abstract truths. The Academy is considered to be the first University and remained open until 529 A.D. when Justinian I closed the school in response to his thought of growing paganism, rather than censorship of Greek philosophy. The Academy flourished for over 900 years due to one man's determination to pay homage to the man who inspired him to seek truth.

Of all of Plato's writings he is most remembered for *The Republic*. Plato describes what he considered was the perfect society in which the ideal government is a meritocracy whereby the best are placed within an elite class as a result of their value. Within this society Plato believed in equality of the sexes, based upon merit, becoming one of the earliest philosophers to advocate the rights of women. The most important aspect of Plato's society is the strict emphasis placed on education, especially the education of the youth. One minor drawback to Plato's society is the elitist view that only the most successful persons within the society shall continue their educational advancement, while those less suited for advancement are assigned to the more menial tasks within a society. The redemption within Plato's work arrives from his designation that the most superior members of society shall not benefit monetarily yet rather obtain their reward through public service.

Plato's most famous concept was the theory of Ideas, a metaphysical concept where ideas are indestructible as opposed to tangible objects. The more real construct was the idea behind an object, because that could never be corrupted. Ideas exist only to expand the mind, while the search for knowledge of abstract principles quenches any desire for sensory pleasure. Plato's use of metaphysics to answer ethical and moral questions influenced medieval thought and culture, providing the basic foundation for social idealism. Plato opposed natural science in favor of moral philosophy and abstract concepts, which in his day lent itself perfect to the burgeoning science of mathematics. In effect Plato became the first mathematical philosopher, applying geometric forms to the heavenly bodies and the universe. Mathematics was reduced to pure thought where wisdom was the highest achievement, creating the new ideal of metaphysical mathematics. In Plato's mind thought reigned above actualized theorems.

Plato's ideal government described in *The Republic* lays the basic groundwork for the emergence of Western political thought. While no one specific government has implemented Plato's ideal model, these concepts resonate in the writings of philosophers who followed Plato, when challenging the structure of their own ruling body. Throughout his lifetime Plato yearned to achieve a balance of harmony through wisdom and knowledge, ideals impressed upon him by Socrates during Plato's formative years. Plato passed away in his sleep in 347 B.C. where, up until his death, he returned the favor Socrates had done for him by teaching the youth of Athens the necessary moral imperatives to achieve these honored ideals, and expected his students to do the same.

90

29

JAMES CLERK MAXWELL

During the latter part of the 18th century the fundamental discovery of electricity occurred. Soon after, electricity was experimented with and later harnessed to benefit technology. In the early stages of this examination process much was learned about electricity yet it was still deemed as an unpredictable field. Science continued to evolve over the years, with electricity and magnetism, the electromagnetic field. This became a cornerstone for advancing the field of astrophysics. The man who was first responsible for deducing the mathematical equations governing electromagnetism was James Clerk Maxwell. Born on June 13th, 1831, in Edinburgh, Scotland, James had a strong desire for knowledge, attending Edinburgh Academy at age 10 where he blossomed in mathematics. At the age of fourteen James wrote a paper on ovals where he defined an ellipse so impressively that the paper was read to the Royal Society of Edinburgh. Continuing to distinguish himself at school in mathematics and natural philosophy Maxwell obtained a fellowship from Trinity College in Cambridge, where he graduated with a degree in mathematics in 1854. It was during his early days at Cambridge where Maxwell began to examine the quantitative nature of electricity and magnetism.

The following year, after the death of his father in 1856, Maxwell examined the motion of the rings of the planet Saturn. The problem arising with Saturn was how the ring system held its stability, and through mathematical analyses Maxwell theorized that the rings consisted of numerous small solid particles, which were independent satellites. As a result of these calculations Maxwell was able to formulate an advanced theory on the motion of molecules within gases. Maxwell merged the atomic theory of matter with the kinetic theory of heat to formulate the kinetic theory of gases. This theory, evolving the basic theories of thermodynamics, altered the flow of molecular movement within gases, adjusting previously assumed temperature shifts into a statistical model. Using statistics Maxwell created a formula, called 'the Maxwell distribution', which identifies what precise portion of molecules will be moving within a specified gas. The statistical formula is applicable to any recorded temperature or velocity and has yet to be disproved in any circumstance. Maxwell developed numerous laws regarding gases, yet the monumental aspect of his theory was that accurate predictions could be made using the statistical model, applicable within many branches of physics.

Maxwell's most noted fame comes from his work on electricity and magnetism. Advancing upon the theories of electricity Maxwell was able to develop four equations, which unified the previously separate field of electricity and magnetism into a combined field of electromagnetism. First released in Maxwell's 1873 book *Electricity and Magnetism*, these four basic laws provided order to a previously muddled system of theories and suppositions that would only work under certain particular circumstances. The equations showed that oscillations, known as electromagnetic waves, were responsible for producing an electromagnetic field, whereby he was able to provide an accurate model that was now able to predict electrical phenomena. An important discovery from Maxwell's laws was that light was a part of the electromagnetic field, consisting of the basic oscillations that govern electromagnetism. This breakthrough became the founding principle within the field of optics. Maxwell's theoretical predictions regarding electromagnetism were later corroborated and these conclusions were utilized as the primary principles behind early electronics.

Along with his work on thermodynamics and electromagnetism Maxwell is considered to have authored the founding theory leading toward the field of cybernetics. His paper ushered in the establishment of mathematical control and systems theory, a necessary aspect for advanced communications and transportation, including space travel. Maxwell's experiments with color vision proved the limitations of the human retina to only process the three primary colors. This discovery enabled him to produce the first color photograph in 1861. His work with electromagnetism also has implications within the field of astrophysics, as the electromagnetic waves are shown to spread in an outward motion through space, creating a mathematical design that may predict astronomical abnormalities affecting the solar system. James Clerk Maxwell has been described as the greatest physicist of his era, despite garnering little or no fame from his work, which later shaped thought and developed principles in numerous diverse fields. Known primarily as a scientist, Maxwell was actually a mathematical physicist, yet even more of a dreamer, grounded in reality.

94

28

ADAM SMITH

The elimination of Feudalism in Europe over an extended period of time opened the door to advancements in science, technology and more importantly the emergence of a middle class. One system of political economy was set up to increase wealth through the exportation of goods, known as mercantilism. Adapting this theory to meet a changing environment, Adam Smith created a capitalist approach to attaining economic prosperity. Smith was born on June 5th, 1723, in the small town of Kirkcaldy, Scotland. His father was the comptroller of customs, yet died prematurely before Adam was born. Adam's mother came from a family of wealthy landowners. When Smith was fourteen, he attended Glasgow University studying moral philosophy, graduating from Glasgow University, at the age of seventeen and was awarded a scholarship to attend Balliol College at Oxford, in London, England.

By 1746 Oxford had become obsolete to Smith and he would soon return to Edinburgh. He sharpened his early theories while leading public lectures in Edinburgh regarding the basics of rhetoric and economics. The famous Scottish philosopher and economist David Hume, twelve years Smith's senior, became one of Smith's closest friends and associates, becoming a major influence on his work. Smith began to gain notice for his theories and lectures, and was appointed the professor of logic at Glasgow University in 1751. Smith transferred to the moral philosophy department, lecturing on such varied topics as ethics and rhetoric. These lectures included preliminary aspects of economic theory as relating to political endeavors. Smith's early work focused on moral elements rather than economic, eventually displayed in Smith's 1759 work '*The Theory of Moral Sentiments*'.

In 1764 Smith gave up lecturing to tutor Henry Scott, the 3rd Duke of Buccleuch. The next two years saw Smith and Scott travel extensively throughout France and Switzerland. During these travels Smith came into contact with important French philosophers and revolutionaries in preparation for a major shift in French politics. Tutoring the young Duke would be an important step in the life of Adam Smith as it awarded him a life pension for his service. This pension allowed Smith to retire to Kirkcaldy in 1766, where he began work on his famous 1776 treatise '*An Inquiry Into the Nature and Causes of the Wealth of Nations'*. Smith accepted the post of Commissioner of Customs in 1778, passing away twelve years later on July 19th, 1790.

The 1776 work by Smith assimilated prior political economic theories, restructuring them into a comprehensive model that rejected the erroneous while simultaneously exalting the accurate aspects. This is not to say that Smith's theory was unoriginal. The exact opposite is true. Never before had someone organized economic theory into a perfectly workable model, thus forming the beginnings of capitalism. Smith's system placed high values on free trade to ensure economic security while also stressing individualism as a major facet to a regulating market. On the other hand Smith strongly devalued governmental interference with regards to high tariffs and the maintenance of a surplus, essentially denouncing classical mercantilism. Smith believed the role of government within the boundaries of economy was to provide a basis for all members of society to produce within their specific economic system. A direct result of this arises within Smith's prototype of the division of labor, which yielded a significant gain in prosperity.

The use of the individual as selfish to foster the economic gains was central to Smith's theory. As a person works to increase their own life and well being, focusing primarily on their own existence, they inadvertently became a key fixture within the mechanism that governs Smith's economic theory. Crucial to this element of Smith's theory is that the economy need not be controlled by the reigning government, yet rather worked as a cohesive unit between government and it's citizens to promote economic harmony. Adam Smith's overall influence and importance reached its zenith in the mid to late nineteenth century, strongly influencing Karl Marx, whose additions and alterations to Smith's model specifically apply to class conflict. Smith's ideas blended into a unified ideal are the foundation for political economics, whereby capitalism has become the main economic principle employed by the majority of industrialized nations. Adam Smith, the man who brought organization to the previously unsystematic world of economics, deserves much of the credit for the growth and expansion of the major manufacturing countries in existence today.

27

YING ZHENG

The Great Wall of China, built in the third century B.C., remains intact today as the only man made structure that can be seen from space. Its erection, once the separate warring regions were conquered and formed together within one cohesive ruling dynasty, safeguarded the kingdom from foreign invaders. Its completion ensured that the cultural and scientific advancements made by China remained within that country for over a millennia. Built under the orders of Ying Zheng, known later by the name Shi Huang-di, or Huang-ti, China's initial evolution into a more structured approach to living began. Born in 259 B.C. to Zhuang Xiang, heir to the throne of the Ch'in dynasty, and a former concubine, or arranged secondary wife. Thirteen years later Zheng's father would become ruler of the Chin dynasty, yet pass away that same year. Only 13 at the time his father died, Zheng's mother and a merchant served as co-regents. In 238 B.C., after a failed revolt against Zheng, he had his mother and the merchant removed as regents and began to take sole charge of his empire.

With the Chin dynasty under his complete control, Zheng undertook the daunting task of expanding his kingdom. Chin, ruled by Zheng, was one of seven warring feudal states within China. In selecting proficient generals Zheng escalated the battles against the other feudal states, eventually conquering all other territories by 221 B.C. Zheng now officially declared himself as the sole King of China, bestowing himself with the title of Shi Huang-di, translated as 'the first emperor'. As ruler of the entire country, having conquered all regions opposing him, Zheng implemented numerous programs in an effort toward the further unification of China. To protect his domain, Zheng abolished the feudal system and replaced it with appointed governors for each province. To prevent the possibility of revolt governors were rotated from province to province with two additional appointed officials to ensure provincial loyalty to the emperor. In the extreme case of a revolt, a system of roads were constructed to connect the provinces to the capital city of Xi'an, where Zheng and his Imperial army had the ability to mobilize and thwart any attempted insurgence from individual provinces. As a result China was stabilized as a unified country under authoritarian rule, with for the first time a policy of guidelines governing daily life existing.

The feudal state of Chin was anti-Confucian in their state policy. Prior to the birth of Ying Zheng, the state of Chin had put into practice the Legalist school of philosophy whereby a set of strict laws were required to govern men. The firm nature of the Legalist philosophy employed by Zheng eventually displayed itself in a decree in 213 B.C. Zheng ordered all books that espoused a philosophical approach in direct opposition to the Legalist philosophy burned. Despite this overt act of censorship, Zheng was able to transform China from a religiously philosophical region toward a nation where a unified and codified system of laws was the first step toward technological and scientific advancement on a national scale. Zheng's Legalist philosophy was centered directly against the Confucian school. Confucian scholars were buried alive and no books containing Confucian doctrine were sent to the Imperial library, as other single copies of books on science and technology were during the execution of this decree.

During the existence of the warring feudal states, each state had walls that separated and protected them from invaders. As Zheng commenced expanding his kingdom to the North and the West these walls were interconnected into one continuous wall along the Northern frontier of China, preventing future raids from conquered regions that were not entirely annexed into China. Thus the Great Wall was created, virtually cutting China off from the rest of the world. Additional reforms included a uniform system of weights and measures most notably pertaining to the axle length of wagons. Zheng also standardized both the national currency as well as the written language. Despite numerous assassination attempts as a result of increased taxation Ying Zheng died of natural causes in 210 B.C. The major improvements enacted during Zheng's reign led China away from the teachings of Confucius, yet his tyrannical rule led toward the establishment of Confucianism as the official state philosophy once the Chin dynasty ended in 206 B.C. Despite this establishment of Confucianism by the Han Dynasty, the primary elements of the Legalist philosophy remained and continue to this day, too important to ignore any longer in favor of a wholly rural lifestyle.

26

JOHN LOCKE

The seeds of democracy arose in ancient Greece, but the Greek democratic experiment soon ended with Macedonian monarchy and the emergence of Rome as an empire. Democracy was re-instituted, in concept only, with the signing of the Magna Carta in England in 1215. However, it would be more than four centuries later when the notions of constitutional democracy could no longer be ignored by the Western world, emanating from the mind of John Locke. He was born on August 29th, 1632 in Wrington, Somerset, England, during a time when England was in a tumultuous period. His father fought on the side of the Parliamentarians during the English Civil War, having a distinct impact of the young Locke, who defended the Parliamentary system throughout his lifetime. His general education as a youth stressed the classics, to which he would later publicly criticize for its steadfast emphasis on the past rather than the present or what Locke would influence, the future.

In 1652 Locke entered Christ Church in Oxford, earning his Bachelor's degree in 1656 and his Master's degree in 1658. While at Oxford he was strongly inspired by John Owen who introduced him to the concept of religious freedom, an idea that would inevitably lead Locke on a path toward freedom of thought and the rights of the citizen. Interested in both science and medicine, Locke was elected to the Royal Society and earned his Bachelor's in medicine. He would become family physician to the Earl of Shaftesbury, known politically as a liberal. The two developed a close friendship as a free flow of ideas were exchanged, until Shaftesbury was imprisoned for his beliefs, forcing Locke to leave England in 1683. While away from England, Locke was able to explore his ideas with some of the preeminent thinkers of the day.

Over the following years Locke's views would be made public, albeit the first of which would be published anonymously. This work, *A Letter Concerning Toleration*, posed the clearest and strongest argument to date for the free exercise of religion. Although not the first man to suggest this concept, Locke's line of reasoning helped support the necessity for religious acceptance among all sects of Protestantism. Locke's major goal was to end the tyranny of religious persecution, yet strangely enough he did not allow this toleration to be extended to atheists or Catholics. The letter was written while Locke was in exile in Holland and as a result, an anti-Catholic feeling resonates throughout this work. In actuality Locke displays an entirely prejudiced approach to religions other than his own, yet the tumultuous times promoted religious fanaticism in both Locke and those who opposed him, forcing him into exile. The magnification of Locke's reasoning has allowed his arguments to endure.

The same year, 1690, Locke published a thesis under his own name, *Two Treatises of Government*. This is by far Locke's most famous and influential work, hailed as a masterpiece of political philosophy whereby Locke's fundamental principles form the basis for constitutional democracy. He argued for the basic rights of the individual; life, liberty and property, while limiting governmental autonomy and rejecting the absolute authority of the sovereign body over its citizens. Locke reasoned that the protection of its citizens and their individual property was the primary function of government. *Two Treatises* is a profound argument against absolutism in favor of the inherent rights of the individual. This work strongly influenced the government of numerous nations wishing to implement democracy and continues to act as a guide in the fight against totalitarianism.

Locke's final major work appeared in 1690, titled *An Essay Concerning Human Understanding*. Straying from his recent political texts Locke delved into natural philosophy, exploring the nature and limits of man's ability to obtain and utilize knowledge. Calling on an empiricist approach, Locke saw the mind starting as a blank slate waiting to explore, refuting the long-standing notion of innate awareness in favor of learned experience. It remains as one of the classics of philosophy, to which Locke is credited as inspiring and founding British empiricism. Locke passed away in 1704 later impacting the thought processes of generations to come as his major works still hold their relevance today. Locke's concepts of constitutional democracy influenced the founding fathers of the American Revolution as well as directly impacting the writings of the author of the United States Constitution. These ideas were also the basis for the onset of the French Revolution during that same century, acting upon Locke's central theses. In the age of Enlightenment, there was perhaps no man more enlightened in progressive thought than John Locke.

106

25

MARCO POLO

A faster and more efficient trade route between Europe and the Far East dominated sea travel during the 14th and 15th centuries. Such voyages led to the European discovery and eventual colonization of the New World, in North and South America. The motivation for numerous countries to explore this quicker sea path resulted directly from a late 13th century travel book, written by an Italian merchant, Marco Polo. Thought by some to be the most influential explorer of all time, Polo was born in Venice, Italy in 1254, the son of explorer and merchant Nicolo Polo. Marco's mother passed away while Nicolo was on a nine-year voyage visiting the Middle East and the Orient. At the age of seventeen Marco journeyed with his father and uncle Maffeo to visit the Mongol Empire of Kublai Khan. This journey would take four years to complete, yet last close to twenty-five years.

After traveling through Persia, Afghanistan and a warring region that prompted the return to Venice of two priests accompanying them, they arrived in Mongol China in 1275. Kublai Khan immediately took a liking to them and offered all three Polo men positions within his court. Marco began as an official in Kublai's Privy Council before moving on to the post of inspector of taxes. Thoroughly trusted by Kublai, their loyalty to him allowed them to amass a great deal of wealth. By the 1290's the Polos longed to return home to Venice and an opportunity arose so they left China in 1292, escorting a princess to Persia. They told Kublai that they would continue homeward to Venice after delivering the princess and Kublai reluctantly agreed. The Polos finally reached Venice in 1295 finishing a journey that began twenty-four years earlier.

Marco became a captain for Venice during their battle over maritime trading superiority with Genoa. He was taken prisoner and spent his imprisonment dictating his adventures in the Orient to fellow prisoner Rusticiano de Pisa. At some time between 1298 and 1299 Marco was released and his stories were soon published under the title *A Description of the World*. This landmark work, more commonly known as *The Travels of Marco Polo*, originally published in French, inspired further European explorations. Marco died in 1324 hinting that he had not revealed half of what he had seen while in the court of Kublai Khan. This further increased the intrigue surrounding an unknown region abundant with riches and trade potential.

On Marco Polo's return to Venice, he introduced numerous products into European culture, including ivory, porcelain china, various spices, silk and paper money. The long standing legend that he introduced spaghetti is more lore than actuality. These products, along with the wealth of gold and jewels amassed during their stay captivated the Europeans. As a result, trade expansion with the Orient was necessitated, establishing lucrative trade routes along the way, still in existence today. From an historical standpoint the trade routes opened up due to Marco's written histories led to one of the most important events of medieval Europe, the bubonic plague. Carried by rats bitten by infected fleas, it surfaced in Europe in 1347, on merchant ships returning from the Black Sea, a key link in the newly established trade route to China. The bubonic plague killed about one third of the entire population of Europe, leading in no small part toward the scientific revolution a century later. Due to the unselective nature of the plague, attacking everyone in its path, most notably the clergy, the ideology of the masses would be forever altered, demystifying the aura of the church.

Marco Polo's book endures as the most essential travel book of all time. The Polos were not the first explorers to visit the Far East, yet Marco's book was in fact the first to document the journey. It served as the primary source of information regarding Asia for centuries. The lucid detail regarding the Polo's voyages within this book laid the foundation for the first concise geographical information of that region, with accurate maps of Asia completed due to Marco Polo's work, inspiring future explorative journeys. A new theory hypothesizes that Marco Polo may never have visited China. The adherents of this premise note the exclusion of numerous Mongol and Chinese daily standards including block printing and chopsticks. Conjecture of this nature may add to the furthering of accurate historical knowledge, yet it in no way detracts from the importance that Marco Polo had on medieval Europe as a result of his recorded journeys. His legend endures, whether or not it remains fact or folklore and his travels would leave a lasting impression on the face of European exploration for centuries to come.

24

THOMAS ALVA EDISON

The age old saying, 'necessity is the mother of invention', was never utilized by any man more than Thomas Edison. Throughout his lifetime Edison would come to hold 1,093 patents. Born on February 11th, 1847 in the wheat shipping port of Milan, Ohio, Edison did not immediately succeed in his initial education. An early teacher of Edison assessed his relentless inquisitiveness as selfish and disruptive, going so far as to negatively describe his head as larger than the other students. Edison would be removed from school by his mother and home taught, eventually outgrowing his own parents' knowledge on advanced academic subjects. The local library provided an outlet for the young Edison's mind to grow as he devoured information toward an understanding of the importance of independent study and examination. This also led to an excelled perseverance necessarily required in establishing his inventive genius.

After a stint as a telegraph operator Edison patented his first invention, an electric vote recorder, at the age of 21. His invention however, was deemed impractical due to its efficiency. This step backward for Edison led to an unfortunate understanding, practical invention was focused on necessity rather than mere inspiration. A few years later Edison would invent the first of his successful commercial inventions, an electric stock ticker, sold in order to establish an electrical engineering firm to continue his work. While at this firm Edison made fundamental improvements to the telegraph and the typewriter. His success afforded Edison the opportunity to set up a factory in Menlo Park, New Jersey with the specific design of producing inventions for profit. One of the first inventions produced in Menlo Park, and one that most people do not associate with Edison, was a definitive improvement to the clarity of sound for the recently invented telephone.

The Menlo Park factory is responsible for Edison's two most important inventions, the phonograph and the electric light bulb. The phonograph, or 'talking machine' as Edison called it, mechanically recorded sound on a cylinder wrapped in tinfoil. An electric motor was added in 1878 to improve audio rhythm with another improvement coming years later. Edison's invention led to the invention of the gramophone, which became the customary system in America and Europe. In 1879, Edison's most celebrated invention came to fruition, the incandescent electric light bulb. Edison used a scorched cotton thread as a filament, solving the problem of sustaining long-term productivity. Edison's electric light bulb paved the way for the installation of a centralized electric power station in New York City by 1882. This station became the world's first practical application of both generating and supplying power, including heat and light, which was affordable to the public. As a result a power company directly responsible for this specific purpose was founded.

There is not enough space to list all the noteworthy inventions and patented improvements to pre-existing inventions made by Edison, but a number of them merit discussion. Edison invented the kinetograph, a camera designed to film motion pictures and the kinetoscope, a motion picture projector, leading toward the development of cinematography. Other inventions of note included the mimeograph copier, later to become known as the photocopier, an alkaline nickel-iron storage battery that had increased electrical capacity, an automatic telegraph and wax paper. Despite having a limited knowledge of practical science Edison is credited with discovering the flow of electrons from a heated filament, labeled as the "Edison effect". This principle would later revolutionize the modern science of electronics.

Thomas Edison worked and invented into his eighties, eventually passing away on October 18th, 1931. His partial deafness has led researchers to suggest that his impairness resulted in an adjusted way of thinking, which produced some of the world's most important discoveries. His perseverance is legendary and his stubbornness cost him the Nobel Prize when he refused to share the award with a former co-worker. The invention laboratory at Menlo Park, and later West Orange, New Jersey became an early model for the development of large research facilities in the 20th century. Edison's multiple business ventures, relating to his inventions, and worldwide companies helped launch America as a world industrial power. Thomas Edison is easily considered the greatest inventive genius who ever lived. It is doubtful that anyone will ever topple him from that mountain.

114

23

HERODOTUS

For a long time in human existence history was passed from generation to generation through oral tradition. Writing had existed since the 4th millennium B.C. yet the methodology regarding the transference of history was not polished. It took one of the earliest recorded explorers, Herodotus, to transform written history into an accredited and vital social science. Acknowledged as the 'father of history', Herodotus was born in 484 B.C. in Halicarnassus, Asia Minor, present day Turkey. His early youth was spent visiting the islands and coastline of Asia Minor. He developed his love of history from the oral traditions of times past while on his various travels, which included trips to the three different continents. A critical element to Herodotus' legend derives from his numerous travels. After Herodotus' travels he lived for a number of years in Athens before retiring to the Southern part of Italy, where he played a major role in establishing the colony of Thurii. While living on Thurii it is hypothesized that Herodotus brought all his research together and produced his most renowned work. By this time Herodotus was in the declining years of his life and left behind a legacy that would endure, helping to begin a cultural advancement in Greek history and learning. The date of his death is most commonly dated at 424 B.C. on the colony of Thurii.

Herodotus' main research derives from a mixture of written and oral traditions regarding the past. His primary work, *The Histories*, chronicles the War between the Persian Empire and Greece. His extensive travels in areas East of Greece allowed him to receive a whole picture of the sixth century battle over control of the Middle East. A major setback to such research is the general biases over what exactly took place, viewed dissimilarly by people of differing cultures. Herodotus came up with a theory of revealing all that was told to him, yet analyzing relevant portions to arrive at the most likely truth, while often times offering his own opinion as to the actual validity of the oral and written traditions of various cultures. The compelling factor is that Herodotus understood that he could not be biased himself when scrutinizing traditions of history, yet still needed to sufficiently alter reported facts as they tended to contradict evidence.

One of Herodotus' favorite places was Egypt, perhaps stemming from his early travels along the coast of Asia Minor. Egypt, or Alexandria for that matter, had not become the cultural center for Hellenistic learning as of yet. Knowledge of this region was almost bare until Herodotus provided the Greek world with their first glimpse into a neighboring land they would come to rule over and position their centers of learning. Herodotus reported of the great Pharaoh Khufu from the 26th century B.C., described as a tyrannical pharaoh who oppressed his subjects and forced the building of the Great Pyramid through the use of slave labor. Future historians, who have found records that the Great Pyramid may have been a public works project have recently challenged this description of Khufu, yet due to the length of elapsed time it is difficult to critically argue either position.

Herodotus recorded history as told to him by the inhabitants of a specific region in a more intimate era than the historians and researchers of today. The claims of the people, as told to Herodotus, must have had an element of truth to them, or Herodotus would have inserted his own opinion that this information may be of a suspect nature. After the information was supplied to Herodotus and he revealed it in writing, historians as many as twenty-four centuries later only have begun to form a dissenting opinion, without clear discernable proof to back up their theories.

While written and oral history pre-existed Herodotus it flourished after his landmark work *The Histories*, with major Greek and Roman historians continuing where Herodotus began. Their individual and cumulative work has distinguished each of them as legendary historians, yet it is the work of Herodotus that provided the necessity for written records. The recognition placed upon Herodotus' work paved the way toward Greece becoming a great center of learning. The placement of the Greek library at Alexandria results from the Greek conquests of that area, which in turn resulted from Herodotus' writings on Egypt and the Middle East. The most significant aspect of Herodotus' life and work is that he took the time to visit the areas he wrote about, placing history on an observational level, where it has remained to this day. This first hand observational approach also makes Herodotus a pioneer in the fields of anthropology, archaeology, sociology and geography.

22

WILLIAM II

When discussing the great battles of history, a temporal and often times cultural bias generally exists. World War I, World War II and the Vietnam War are all thrown into the discussion. Even both the Civil and Revolutionary Wars are mentioned. While these battles were incredibly important in shaping 19th and 20th century politics, arguably no battle had a greater impact upon society than the 1066 Battle of Hastings. This battle might never have happened, and by all rights of royal succession should not have occurred. There was one man who took it upon himself, exercising an incredibly weak claim to the English throne, and with some strokes of luck, William II, Duke of Normandy, embarked upon a quest that would shape the future path of Western civilization.

William was the illegitimate son of Robert I, Duke of Normandy, and a tanner's daughter named Herleve or Arlette. The couple never married, which led to later enemies of William to commonly refer to him as "William the Bastard". His father passed away in 1035, at which time William was installed as the new Duke. Once he came of age William displayed his leadership in battle, gaining his first victory in 1046 against his own rebelling Barons, who objected to William's knighthood in 1042, at the young age of 14. While his future battles in Normandy were important for establishing a reputation, it would be one battle in England that altered the shape of Western history.

In 1051, King Edward promised the throne of England, upon his death, to William. William had a weak claim, his great aunt was Edward's mother, and perhaps as a reward for safeguarding Edward in Normandy during tumultuous times in England, William was assured that his claim to the English throne would be enforced. In 1064, William was promised the throne of England, by Harold Godwinson. When Edward died in the beginning of 1066, Harold claimed the throne of England.

On October 14th, 1066, Harold and William met in battle, at Hastings. Harold's army, who had just defeated the Norwegian King Harald Hardrada, was defeated and killed in battle. William was crowned King of England on Christmas Day. Despite the weakness or strength of William's claim to the throne of England, the battle of Hastings would never have occurred without him. The shape of English monarchy was changed forever, and every reigning monarch since William can trace their lineage back to him. An entirely new line of succession in England would exist because of the stubbornness of one individual.

Prior to 1066, England was basically a backwater country. It was constantly invaded by Scandinavian Viking raiders, controlled by Denmark and ruled by a blend of Germanic tribes that had occupied England for centuries, after the departure of Rome. England was tossed back and forth from one marauding power to the next, that is until William took control. From that time after no foreign attacker successfully invaded England. Through William's strong leadership England now became a stable monarchy, eventually growing into the world's strongest empire.

A number of immediate changes occurred as a result of William's invasion. England, which was a blend of Germanic, Celtic and Scandinavian culture, had an immediate infusion of French culture and language thrust upon them. As a result the entire English language was changed, evolving from a barbaric dialect into an advancing vernacular. This would mean extremely little if not for the mere fact that English is the most widely spoken language in the world today, the English that William forged from his own brand of Scandinavian French and existing English.

Other direct changes made by William included the first census, called *The Domesday Book*. This was taken to ascertain the property within the land, centralizing the government under his complete control, while also strengthening it. This allowed England to not only build the foundation of an empire, but also to expand it, once initial revolts were suppressed. All the people were essentially vassals of William, creating an advanced form of Feudalism. Borrowed over from France, where William was a vassal of the French King, this evolved form led to the development of democracy under the *Magna Carta*. The expansion of democracy in Europe can therefore be directly attributed to William. His conquest of England greatly impacted the future path of history. Had he not invaded, the world we know of would be a different place.

21

HAMMU-RAPI

Law is the governing principle behind society. To enforce laws and ensure the evolution and advancement of any society, these laws must be placed in writing for the citizenry to acknowledge and obey or face the established punishments. The oldest set of laws currently known, consisting of seven laws and a minor praise of the King, belongs to Nammu, King of Ur, an ancient city in Mesopotamia, however historians agree that the world's first true legal code belongs to the sixth King of the first dynasty of Babylon, Hammu- rapi, known today as Hammurabi. The date of his birth is uncertain, with some historians placing it as far back as the 21st century B.C., however the general consensus is that Hammurabi's reign began in 1792 B.C., inheriting the throne from his father. From an examination of the length of Hammurabi's reign, until his death in 1750 B.C., this would place him at the minimum of sixty-two years of age upon his death. A speculative date of birth of approximately 1815 B.C. is a reasonable estimate. Hammurabi also inherited a War with the city-state of Larsa, in Sumer. Hammurabi won the War, after an undisclosed, but lengthy period of time. This conquest set in motion the expansion of what would become the Babylonian Empire. Leading his kingdom to victory in this long battle indicates that he was either a gifted warrior or leader or perhaps both, suggesting that he was most likely at least in his twenties upon coming into power.

When Hammurabi came to power Babylon's kingdom stretched 80 miles long and 20 miles wide. The surrounding city-states in Mesopotamia were both culturally and geographically stronger than Babylon, so Hammurabi rebuilt his kingdom from within prior to conquering the surrounding city-states under the control of one empire. At its height, the Babylonian Empire stretched as far as the Persian Gulf and to Assyria, with Babylon becoming a cultural center, comparable to that of Greece and Rome centuries later. Foreign commerce was encouraged as public houses and taverns were built for travelers involved in trade. A class of skilled laborers materialized to meet the demands of an ever-growing market. Masons, carpenters and other laborers initiated a system of apprenticeship, which would become a precursor to the European apprentice-ships employed in the Middle Ages. As business increased the need for institu-tions that safeguarded income arose, resulting in the emergence of independent bankers. Even after Babylon was later conquered the impact of their advanced civilization remained, branching outward into the Western World.

The Code of Hammurabi, a set of laws governing daily life, remains as his most important achievement. Unearthed by French architects in 1902, the code was carved in cuneiform, a wedge shaped script employed by the ancient Babylonians, on a seven-foot high stone slab. Comprised of 282 laws, with evidence of another 35, specifying conduct and enforcing punishment, the code was established on the ancient governing principle of the punishment fitting the crime. As a result the code was viewed as severe, yet this guaranteed civil order in an advancing society, and Hammurabi is remembered as originating order out of chaos during a turbulent time in ancient history. This became the first instance where laws were codified for the citizenry to publicly view, ensuring that punishments could not be spontaneously determined at the impulse of the King. This classification of laws structuralized the ruling government, which afforded the commoners individual rights within a community. This codification of law became the forerunner for contemporary legal systems utilized with an advancing society.

Hammurabi was not only the King of Babylon, considered its greatest ruler, he was also the chief priest of the society. His pioneering legal code governed religious life as well, yet unlike other previous despotic rulers Hammurabi was open to freedom of religion, only specifying that the laws of the code be followed. Hammurabi was therefore a visionary, separating church from state in the realization that law above beliefs must govern a society. During the reign of Hammurabi, mathematicians introduced the mathematical concept of algorithms for solving problems, temples and roads were built, libraries were opened to advance knowledge, and the irrigation process was improved by the construction of canals. Countless numbers of societies, countries and govern-ments owe a gratitude to the innovations created by Hammurabi. Although his rule included a series of battles to unite his kingdom, his multilateral approach to daily life cements his legacy as an honest and tolerant intellectual, unfortunately born way before an era that could fully appreciate him.

20

ALEXANDER III

What constitutes an empire? An empire consists of a vast area of lands held under the control of one ruling body, usually ruled over by one individual. Some empires throughout history have been smaller than others but have produced a far greater impact on world history than those of larger area. Amount of land controlled by an empire does not necessarily correlate to impact yet in the 4th century B.C. the man controlling the empire that had conquered more of the known world than any other previous empire, Alexander the Great, was also able to substantially shape the scope of future history.

Alexander was born into a noble family in the summer of 356 B.C., to Philip II, King of Macedon, in Northern Greece. Philip II was a brilliant leader and warrior uniting all of Greece under Macedonian rule. The Greek philosopher Aristotle, who instilled in Alexander a sense of culture and bred in him a passion for knowledge, supervised Alexander's education. His other education was on the battlefield, where his bravery displayed itself. This dualistic education made Alexander the multi-cultural leader he would later become, ascending to the throne upon Philip's death in 336 B.C. Throughout Greece it was believed that the death of Philip II would allow Greece to escape from Macedonian rule.

As talented of a warrior and leader as Philip II was Alexander was that much better in both categories. Alexander's courage and leadership prevailed when he reunited all of Greece under Macedonian rule within two years. With Greece under his complete control Alexander sought to accomplish what his father always desired, conquering Persia. Alexander marched into Asia Minor and defeated Persian forces on his way to meet Persian King Darius III on the field of battle at Issus, in 333 B.C. Although heavily outnumbered by the Persian Army, Alexander led his troops to victory earning complete control over Asia Minor. Alexander continued to extend his empire, occupying and controlling all of the current day Middle East, then entering Egypt, seizing control without a fight. Alexander continued eastward invading and winning decisive victories in Afghanistan, successfully opening up the path to India. He entered Western India and conquered the Punjab, but his troops refused to continue into eastern India. Alexander complied and his army marched back into Persia, conquering all who opposed him on the journey. Despite the obvious ambition exhibited by

Alexander his empire never extended into Eastern India, as he passed away from a stomach illness in 323 B.C., while in Babylon, modern day Iraq.

Alexander's gift to the world was the sharing of cultures between nations. Alexander immediately immersed himself into foreign culture. He would have a strong impact on the cultural expansion of Eastern Europe, the Middle East, and Western Asia. The cultural merging of his empire demonstrates an advanced perception of the world, while most leaders believed cultures other than their own were barbaric and inferior. Alexander's efforts paved the way for worldwide cultural expansion. Alexander founded more than twenty new cities, most notable the cultural learning center of the ancient world, Alexandria, named for him in Egypt. Having a thirst for and love of knowledge instilled upon him at an early age by Aristotle, Alexander set up a multi-cultural epicenter for the advancement of knowledge in Alexandria, where the great library was built, which housed all the relevant and innovative knowledge in the world up until two fires may have lost this knowledge forever. On his journeys historians and scholars were commonplace, gathering and extrapolating historical data to institute a cross-cultural advancement of learning.

While war and conquest was a direct objective of Alexander, he had the sophisticated intellect to realize the necessity for knowledge, understanding that advanced thought leads to an advanced society, which Alexander attempted to create wherever he went. With Alexander's untimely death at the age of 33 it is difficult to speculate how far his empire would have reached. His plans for invading Arabia and controlling the entirety of Asia obviously would have altered the course of history, perhaps stalling the arrival of the Roman Empire. Over the course of years of historical discussion Alexander the Great has been likened to Napoleon, or more recently Hitler. Conversely he has also been equated with many Generals who have halted tyranny. Time shall continue this discussion yet even Alexander understood, by an influx of foreign culture and ideas, that there is more than one side to every story.

130

19

NAPOLEONE BUONAPARTE

At the end of the 18th century France was in a state of economic and social disorder. The excesses of the wealthy ruling class led to revolution and a military state. A leader emerged who would attempt to restore France to glory and ultimately endeavor to control the entirety of Europe. Often called the *"human God of War"*, Napoleon Bonaparte was born on August 15th, 1769, on the island of Corsica. Just over a year prior to Napoleon's birth, Corsica had been sold to France by Genoa making Napoleon French by birth. However, Napoleon started out as a Corsican nationalist with an ardent hatred for the French. His father, a lawyer, descended from Corsican nobility, whose ambition for climbing the political and social ladder facilitated Napoleon's entrance into a military academy and later the *Ecole Royale Militaire* in Paris in 1784. Upon his graduation, Napoleon became a second lieutenant, at the age of sixteen. France was about to embark on an historic period of change, allowing Napoleon's own ambition and military prowess to emerge.

Stationed on Corsica during his early military career, Napoleon's first noteworthy victory came in 1793 at Toulon, one of the few times Napoleon would be victorious in battle against the English, earning him the rank of Brigadier General. Successfully maneuvering through political turmoil in France Napoleon led the French forces to victory against the Austrian army in Italy. After returning in 1799 from Egypt Napoleon became a member of the ruling triumvirate, ruling France as a dictatorship. In 1804 Napoleon was crowned Emperor and began his ground domination of Europe. The following year Napoleon, coming off another naval defeat at the hands of the English, won an overwhelming victory over Russia and Austria, defeated Prussia in 1806 and Austria again in 1807 and 1809. Napoleon invaded Russia in 1812, a defeat that would prompt his first exile from France. Spurned on by Russia's victory Austria and Prussia defeated Napoleon in 1813. He returned to France in 1815 but was defeated at Waterloo by a united European army and exiled to St. Helena as a prisoner of the English, dying six years later, in 1821, of stomach cancer.

In 1798, Napoleon decided to attack the British Empire, focusing on their colonies in India, Syria and most importantly Egypt. Napoleon dominated on land but was thoroughly defeated by the English at sea, giving England complete control of the Mediterranean Sea while refocusing Napoleon on the ground conquest of Europe. Napoleon returned to France after the crushing naval defeat yet an important historical event occurred as a result of the French invasion of Egypt. In 1799 a black basalt stone was discovered in Rosetta, a small city on the outskirts of Alexandria. The stone had three distinct written scripts; whereupon the eventual deciphering of in 1822 would lead to finally understanding Egyptian hieroglyphics, gathering an appreciation for an advanced culture whose knowledge included astronomy, medicine and mathematics while still enjoying a passion for artistic endeavors. Finding the Rosetta Stone ushered in the inauguration of modern Eurasian archaeology.

When Napoleon assumed control, France was still reeling from the effects of the French Revolution. Through his leadership France evolved from a revolutionary republic into an emerging empire. Napoleon transformed the economy, restructured the educational system and created a lasting legislative legacy, an ingenious legal system called the *Code Napoleon*, a modernized structure of civil laws that has endured, albeit with standard modifications, within France to the present. Promoting social equality while denouncing the aristocratic birthright, Napoleon's civil codes assured French citizens of the legal and social improvements that embodied the French Revolution. Providing the model for a structuralized society during a time of constant unrest, Napoleon's code became the archetype for numerous other European countries' legal systems.

Napoleon Bonaparte did not limit himself to influencing the course of modern Europe. His influence extended to North and South America. The Louisiana Purchase in 1803 began the westward expansion of the United States leading toward their emergence as a world power, while Spain's involvement in the Napoleonic Wars severely weakened their stronghold in South America eventually leading to liberation from Spanish rule. Considered to be one of the greatest military tacticians, at the height of his success Napoleon ruled over an empire as vast as the Greek empire of Alexander the Great, yet his impetuous lust for power ultimately led to his downfall.

18

MARTIN LUTHER

During the Dark and Middle Ages challenging the power of the Roman Catholic Church resulted in persecution and often times painful execution. The Church's influence extended to a wide variety of issues including matters of science, yet they consistently exerted their power over religious doctrine. Early attempts at reformations failed due to suppression by the powerful Catholic Church, yet a German monk named Martin Luther made the first breakthrough in successfully challenging the authority of the Catholic Church. Born on November 10th, 1483, in the small town of Eisleben, Germany, Luther received a strong education, becoming a devout student, enrolling at the University of Erfurt at the age of seventeen. One year later he earned his Bachelor's degree and by 1505 Luther had obtained a Master's degree, with the intention of studying law. A life affirming change occurred the following year and Luther abandoned his studies to enter the monastery. Ordained as a Catholic priest in 1507, he was assigned a lecturing position while attaining his bachelor's degree in theology.

As Luther continued his work in theology, he developed an alarming negative sense of his own self worth, arriving at the only true solution to remedy this problem; salvation through faith. On a trip to Rome, Luther observed the absolution of sins in exchange for monetary concessions. This selling of indulgences infuriated Luther and set the course for one of the most important stages in European history. On October 31st, 1517, Luther nailed his *'95 theses'* to the door of a Church in Wittenburg, Germany, wherein he denounced the selling of indulgences by the Catholic Church as well as criticizing the overtly human practices of the church in general. Luther personally sent a copy of his *'95 theses'* to the Archbishop of Mainz, whom he directly accused of fraudulent activity. This indictment insured the alerting of the Catholic Church of Luther's claims and grievances. No small-scale suppression of Luther's theses could take place as a result.

Unlike previous attempts at a reformation of the Catholic Church, this endeavor had a number of positive elements in its favor. Due to the advent of the printing press, Luther's document could be circulated throughout a widespread area as opposed to the prior reformations, which were locally sustained and easily suppressed by the Church. This somewhat forced the hand of the Church in dealing with Luther. In 1521 Luther was ex-communicated by Pope Leo X as a heretic and forbidden protection under the law, to be known as the Edict of Worms. Still unwilling to recant his beliefs against the Catholic Church, Luther was hidden by German nobles and princes for his own protection. Luther's beliefs, outlined in his '95 theses', had become adopted and supported in Germany mainly by those who had tired of the dominance and extremist rule of the Catholic Church. Other factors included a contemptuous view against the Holy Roman Church on the part of those German nobles who protected and safeguarded Luther for interfering in governmental policies. Originally created as an attack against the greed of the Catholic Church, the Protestant Reformation was kept alive in Germany due to a political and civil struggle against the tyranny of the Church.

Along with the Scientific and Industrial Revolutions, the Protestant Reformation was one of the most significant events in European History. As a result of Martin Luther's opinionated views on eternal salvation through mere faith, Christianity was virtually divided. This division created a number of severe religious wars in Europe, for centuries to come. As ordinary citizens were given the opportunity for religious freedom of thought, ample chances for intellectual and cultural advancements were finally a possibility. Religious freedoms such as these led toward European settlements in North America and the idea that long-standing church doctrine directly contradicted the development of intellectually advanced thought. Progress over oppression was now possible.

Martin Luther's main concern was to serve God in the only way he believed possible, through absolute faith. His translation of the Bible into German allowed non-aristocrats that same opportunity, which had previously been suppressed as a tool to control those who could not directly benefit the church. Prior to his death in 1546 Luther displayed a severe degree of anti-Semitism that echoed his entire life. Luther was steadfast in his own beliefs, unwilling to accept any opposing ideas. This stubborn hypocrisy did allow for further religious freedom and advancement yet was not without its future draw-backs. Following Luther's cue, Germany would later become an absolutist nation where opposing thought and ultimately, opposing races, were silenced and harshly dealt with.

17

CHING HUNG

Written communication has been around since the middle of the fourth millennium B.C. Originally words or symbols were carved into rocks, walls or stone slabs. The earliest advancement was a woven mat of reeds called papyrus, later advanced by the Greeks who used parchment, made from animal skins. While significantly better than writing on stone, papyrus and parchment limited production capability ensuring that multiple copies of important documents were a lengthy process or often times sacrificed. A more efficient method of producing material for the written word was needed and although not actually inventing what is commonly referred to today as paper, a Chinese court official named Ching Hung, recognized today as Tsai Lun, developed the much improved process for creating paper. Born in the Hunan Province in approximately 48 A.D., Tsai Lun grew up in a town known for its abundance of metals and ores, bringing the small region of Kuei-Yang to the attention of the central government of China and starting Tsai Lun on the road to his future career.

Tsai Lun served as a liaison to the Privy Council in 75 A.D., managing the household for the Royal family. The death of the Emperor in 77 A.D. prompted the promotion of Tsai Lun to political advisor. In 89 A.D. Tsai Lun helped overthrow the reigning Empress and restore the throne to Emperor Han Ho Ti. He was rewarded by an appointment as the Chief of the Imperial Supply Department. While in this office Tsai Lun's duties included sword and furniture making, but as an overseer of the Imperial Library he noticed the large stacks of heavy books and the disorder produced from their storage. This provided the impetus for creating a more efficient form of paper. In 105 A.D. Tsai Lun presented Emperor Han Ho Ti with the first samples of the improved paper.

After the death of Emperor Han Ho Ti that same year the ruling Empress abolished the Imperial Supply Department and dismissed Tsai Lun from his Imperial duties. For his long-standing service Tsai Lun was made Lord of Lung Ting in 114 A.D. The death of the Empress in 121 A.D. set about a series of events that induced Tsai Lun to take a bath, dress in his best robes and drink a mixture of wine and poison, ending his own life.

The commonly held belief that Tsai Lun invented paper is a misnomer.

Samples of paper have been unearthed dating back to between 49 and 8 B.C. and the first systematic dictionary in China, written in 69 A.D., held an entry for paper. While Tsai Lun could therefore have not invented paper, he must be accredited with the improvement of papermaking, using finely beaten fibers from tree bark in a solution of water and adding a mucilaginous substance. The material was drained of water and dried thus producing paper, the same basic method as is in use today. These secrets of papermaking were guarded in China until the 6th or 7th century when they passed to Korea. In 751 a group of Chinese papermakers were captured by the Arabs and forced to reveal their secrets. These secrets eventually passed along to the European community as a byproduct of the Crusades in the late 12th century. This efficient method of papermaking led toward the mass production of books and manuscripts in the European community directly leading toward the necessity for the invention of the printing press during the Renaissance when a multitude of progressive thought was produced. This invention paved the way for the scientific revolution due to the increased accessibility of information, of which Tsai Lun's efficient method of papermaking is a major contributing factor.

Prior to Tsai Lun's advancement in the art of papermaking books in China were made of bamboo, wood and silk. Both bamboo and wood were extremely bulky and hard to carry. As a result, much fewer books were produced. Silk was lighter then either bamboo or wood, but enormously expensive, adding to the underproduction of books, limiting the advancement of knowledge to only the wealthy and powerful. Tsai Lun's economical procedure greatly increased the production of paper and books. This helped make China an advancing civilization due to their accomplishments and cultural developments far exceeding those of the western world. Once the paper originally made by Tsai Lun reached the Western world, Europe was able to make similar cultural advances in civilization to that of China, in a relatively short period of time. Papermaking, using the bark of a tree as its foundation might have ultimately been discovered; yet credit to this major advancement belongs specifically to one man, Tsai Lun. His unique vision greatly changed the world from a society focusing on mere beliefs toward hypothetical and eventually proven thought, encompassing an entire range of old and pioneering subjects.

16

ALBERT EINSTEIN

Theoretical physics had reached its apex in the late 17th century when Isaac Newton produced a universal working model. That model thoroughly governed physics until the early 20th century when a Swiss patent clerk named Albert Einstein developed an interestingly groundbreaking hypothesis that would alter the scope of theoretical physics. Perhaps the greatest theoretical mind of the 20th century Einstein was born on March 14th, 1879 in Ulm, Germany. The family moved to Munich during the following year where Einstein would begin his education. Einstein was not an early success primarily due to his dislike of the educational system's inflexibility, emphasizing the classics. At age seventeen he was admitted to the Swiss Polytechnic Institute, concentrating his studies on physics. In 1901 Einstein became a naturalized Swiss citizen and took the post of technical assistant in the Swiss Patent Office. Einstein would obtain his Doctorate Degree from the University of Zurich in 1905. This was the same year that introduced Albert Einstein's genius to the world.

Einstein published three papers in 1905, the most noteworthy of which was to be known as the theory of special relativity. Special relativity states that the speed of light does not change depending on the velocity of an observer, indicating that time and space turn out to be a united frame of reference. By rejecting the accepted concept of absolute space and time, postulated by Newton, and the premise that motion can be defined in unconditional terms, Einstein provided a unified description of both the law of electromagnetism and mechanics. Einstein's theory explained how scientific measurements are relative, yet unlike his predecessors Einstein was able to express this theory in accurate mathematical terms. A further account of this theory included the equation $E = mc$ (*squared*), which indicates that converting even small amounts of matter results in overwhelming amounts of energy released. This equation clarified the enormous amount of energy discharged by both the Sun and from nuclear reactions.

With Einstein's credentials rising within the academic community he advanced his general theory of relativity in 1915, dealing specifically with gravitational forces and discrepancies within Newtonian theory. He postulated that gravity exists due to the curvature of space, corroborated by the existence of mass relative to the speed of light. Basing his original hypothesis on logic rather than empiricism, Einstein was able to express these ideas in mathematical form where accurate predictions could be formed and tested. Astronomical observation conducted in 1919 proved the general theory of relativity. To this day there has been no contradictory data to even partially disprove this specific theory. As with numerous theories there are exceptions to the rule, however, Einstein's general theory of relativity lacks any exceptions that would appear to challenge its validity.

Einstein was awarded the Nobel Prize in 1921 for his 1905 paper providing explanations of the photoelectric effect. When light struck specific metals it knocked electrons loose. Einstein was able to observe and describe mathematically, that two factors of light, color and brightness, were directly responsible for the speed and amount of electrons released. The important implication from these computations was that light was composed of a stream of particles as opposed to waves, the prevailing opinion of physicists prior to Einstein's work. Einstein's investigations on the properties of light were the foundation for the photon theory of light as well as becoming a vital element of quantum physics.

The basis of Albert Einstein's work on relativity paved the way for advancements through reliable explanations of the cosmos, including the fascinating notion that the universe is expanding to quantum hypotheses that will lead us into the 21st century. For over 25 years he worked on a unified field theory to unite physics but was eventually unable to prove his equations, publishing his theory in spite of this because he strongly believed it was possible. Einstein was instrumental in the United States developing the first atomic bomb, although not an active participant in its creation. Later Einstein became involved in the abolition of nuclear weapons. Albert Einstein passed away on April 18th, 1955, in Princeton, New Jersey, where he had received a lifetime appointment after moving to the United States. Einstein altered the way academics approached science, creating a sophisticated approach to explain what was long thought unexplainable. No one argues the undeniable value or effect Albert Einstein had upon future progress in physics and all theoretical and applied sciences.

15

ANTOINE LAURENT LAVOISIER

The junior science of chemistry achieved credible status during the latter part of the 18th century with the isolation and discovery of numerous elements. As with many burgeoning sciences a wide range of theories are offered attempting to govern them. One theory was presented and widely accepted as fact, despite its unproven status, until an ambitious Frenchman named Antoine Lavoisier decided to disprove this major theory. On August 26th, 1743, the man who would revolutionize the world of chemistry was born in Paris, France. His father was a lawyer and his mother, who died when Antoine was young, originated from a wealthy family. Her sister was basically in charge of raising the young Antoine. For close to a decade Antoine attended the College Marazin, known for its excellence in scientific study. Following in his father's footsteps, he studied law earning a degree in jurisprudence. Antoine, however, had other ideas about his future career.

The world of science became a passion for Antoine starting with the field of botany, eventually moving onto chemistry. The field of chemistry was far different than the times of Paracelsus combining chemistry and alchemy to the field of medicine. Scientists were discovering the essential chemical elements, thus exploding the field of chemistry into the mainstream. Despite their discoveries a general lacking of organization existed within this field. Lavoisier changed all this by establishing the first fundamental working theory of combustion merely by deflating its greatest governing myth, a theory of combustion using a hypothetical substance called phlogiston. Phlogiston was offered as the explanation for why elements burn, with phlogiston released into the air upon combustion. Through experimentation Lavoisier came to the belief that the existence of phlogiston was nothing more than an incorrect myth. His theory on the conservation of mass regarding the non-existence of phlogiston was not immediately accepted among his peers until his 1789 book, *Elements of Chemistry*. This work unmistakably presented the hypothesis in such a convincing systematic theory that it had to be accepted, mainly because it was both accurate and easily understandable.

Due to the receipt of a wealthy inheritance Lavoisier was able to devote the majority of his time toward experimentation. As a result he joined a group some time before 1770 called the *Ferme General*, a private association responsible for the collection of taxes for the King of France. His involvement with this company, albeit minimal, would eventually prompt his arrest during the latter part of 1793, because of the French Revolution and the *Ferme General's* complete and utter detestation by the new regime. Despite numerous pleas to pardon this great genius, Lavoisier was guillotined on May 8th, 1794 along with the other twenty-seven members of the *Ferme General*.

Lavoisier worked on a number of significant areas within the field of chemistry and overall scientific discovery. These varied fields encompassed street lighting, water purification, gunpowder production and farming. During his experimentation with elements, Lavoisier made significant contributions to the field of physiology, correctly theorizing the internal process of respiration. Chemical discoveries continued during this time as two years prior to his famous 1789 treatise, Lavoisier devised the first practical system of nomenclature for chemical elements, allowing scientists to accurately describe newly found elements within the scientific community, so other scientists could understand and advance their work. This basic system of chemical categorization remains as the primer for the periodic table of elements in use today.

Lavoisier's work with gunpowder production would have a direct effect on the Revolutionary War, allowing the United States to secure a victory. Lavoisier's efficient methods resulted in a surplus of gunpowder prompting trading with the United States, helping to change the tide of the war in their favor against England. The functional system of chemical nomenclature, as well as the proved law of the conservation of mass, altered the way chemistry was viewed during a time of fascinating discovery. This organizational system eventually led toward the establishment of the metric system, yet more importantly, fostered the advancement of a field through a definitive and convenient terminology. These innovations designate Lavoisier as the father of modern chemistry. In actuality, Lavoisier took a pseudo science governed by mere hypothesis and evolved it into an actual science via factual experimentation, specified analysis and designation of interpretive data.

14

SOLON

The ancient world was ruled by Emperors, Pharaohs and Kings, most of who reigned under a dictatorship. While some were benevolent more were authoritarian, forcing their own will upon the subjects of their kingdom. With the emergence of more and more societies the necessity for a change in the ruling structure was imperative to further develop civilization. One of the most important political principles, the establishment of democracy, is directly attributable to the Athenian lawmaker Solon. Born in Athens, around 639 B.C. to a wealthy family, during a time of growing agitation within an emerging middle class, his early career is almost non-existent in the historical records. It is a safe assumption that Solon excelled in his studies that most assuredly would have included classical literature and the law.

One of the first documented accounts of Solon's life takes place around 596 B.C. Solon became an avid supporter for the cause of Athens in the war against Megara for possession of the island of Salamis, gathering a troop and commanding them to victory. As a result of his leadership Solon was revered and the following year he was appointed as the sole Archon by the leading aristocrats. As Archon, Solon was placed in charge of Athens, responsible for the governing and further development of the city. His first duty was to examine and repeal the cruel and harsh laws set forth by the Athenian statesmen Draco in 621 B.C. These reforms, instituted by Solon in 594 included the abolition of serfdom, altering the Athenian constitution to provide limited power to landowners, adjusting the citizenship requirements to include common citizens and introducing a new sector of the people into direct governmental participation according to economic classes. He further created a system of checks and balances within the government to suppress revolt and aristocratic oppression against the lesser classes. Solon traveled for a number of years only to return to Athens to see warring factions within the government he set up. After numerous attempts to reconcile these issues Solon withdrew from political life, eventually passing away on the island of Cyprus at the age of eighty.

A minor aside to Solon's legacy as lawmaker is that he is recorded as the first person to speak about the lost continent of Atlantis. Plato retold a story, based on oral tradition, handed down from generations by Solon. Solon had heard of the lost continent while on a journey to Egypt, as the legend proclaims. The impact that the Atlantis legend has had upon archaeology and culture is deeply underestimated. A recent resurgence of Atlantean theory throughout the 20th century evolved out of major archaeological discoveries, coupled with the rebirth of an interest in Greek mythology emanating from Solon has led to the expansion of knowledge from times past. The search for Atlantis is more than mere archaeology. It is an exploration into myth and mysticism that continues today, fully encompassing the lives of those who undertake the search for this fabled location.

Solon's principal influence comes from his reforms of Draconian law. In abolishing serfdom and pseudo-slavery to aristocracy, establishing entitlement to proprietors and allowing governmental participation within the lesser classes, Solon is solely responsible for instituting the earliest form of constitutional democracy. The Athenian city-state flourished as a result of Solon's law reforms and a cultural epicenter was created that developed the greatest minds of the time. The democratic experiment slowly faded away in favor of monarchy, yet those ideals and values would eventually return to the world and form the basis for the large percentage of currently existing governments.

The role of government in providing for its citizenry is paramount to the development of any society. The basic fundamental principle behind a successful evolving society is democracy. As civilizations continue to advance democracy becomes a dominant factor in that progression. With his legal reforms Solon set forth in motion the ideology that would eventually change the modern world, more than twenty-two centuries after their initial establishment. Known as one of the 'seven sages', Solon would create a strategy for eradicating civil unrest, one that would endure the test of time. Democratic forms of government returned to display the supreme benefits to society and civilization. Solon's importance to the legal and governmental advancement to civilization today is therefore immeasurable. Unfortunately Solon would not be able to witness his creation come to its true fruition, as is generally the case with those who institute greatness.

13

MIKOLAJ KOPERNIK

The geocentric theory of the universe, where the Earth is considered the center of the universe, with all other planets, moons and stars revolving around the Earth, was formulated in ancient times. Its most notable propagator was Ptolemy, whose affiliation with the Roman Catholic Church allowed the geocentric universe theory to govern the belief structure regarding the solar system for centuries. A Polish Astronomer named Mikolaj Kopernik did not originate the heliocentric theory of the universe, accurately describing the Sun as the center of our solar system. This existed in the minds of some ancient Greeks, Aristarchus of Samos proposed as the initial hypothesizer however, it took the courage, insight and analytical skills of that part time Polish astronomer to demonstrate that a geocentric model was in fact incorrect. Kopernik, known by his westernized name Nicolas Copernicus, was born in Torun, Poland, in 1473. His father passed away when Copernicus was only ten, at which time his maternal uncle became his full time guardian.

In 1491 Copernicus attended the University of Krakow, where his first interest in astronomy surfaced. Astronomy however, would become a passion opposed to a profession. Copernicus traveled to Italy in 1496 and studied a wide range of subjects including philosophy, mathematics, medicine and law, ultimately receiving a doctorate in canon law in 1503. By 1506, Copernicus had finished his university studies, returning home to care for his uncle, who had risen to the position of Bishop of Ermland, where Copernicus was elected a canon of Frauenberg Cathedral. As this post was designated a non-religious position, Copernicus was allowed the freedom to practice a variety of pursuits, actively taking part in matters of military defense and the resulting peace negotiations, restructuring national currency but most notably focusing on astronomical endeavors.

Copernicus did not have the advantage of a telescope for his cosmological observations, while having the added detriment of frequently dense weather conditions to prevent a consistent stream of astronomical data. This did not deter Copernicus who utilized a turret on a tower as an observatory, collecting his data with astonishingly archaic instrumentation. One year later Copernicus began distributing a summary analysis of his cosmological beliefs.

This small manuscript would never see widespread publication during Copernicus' lifetime, and this has prompted theorists to suggest Copernicus' hesitance to publish was due to a reluctance to embarrass or contradict the accepted church doctrine of a geocentric universe. That assumption is incorrect. In 1530 Copernicus completed his revolutionary masterpiece, but still hesitated to publish. His reluctance was based strictly on what he believed to be limited or insufficient data. Copernicus insisted his model have strong mathematical data to support a hypothesis planning to usurp the 1300-year-old accepted presumption. Continuing to collect further observational information Copernicus' ideas were eventually published in 1543. Shortly afterward, on May 24th, 1543, he would pass away.

Copernicus formulated the heliocentric model of the universe due to observed anomalies in planetary distances, which were not explained under the Ptolemaic geocentric model. Heliocentric theory perfectly explained why certain planets varied in brightness due to their proximity to the Earth. Through a mathematical pattern of retrograde motion, planets closer to the Sun underwent smaller orbits, justifying planetary distances resulting in assorted patterns of clarity. Copernicus' model, however, did not completely portray what is currently known about the cosmos, yet became the basic groundwork for these advancements in astronomy and science during the 17th century. His work embodied the dawn of modern astronomy and the establishment of modern science.

Nicolaus Copernicus embodied the Renaissance, a man who prospered in medicine, science, economics and the arts, translating poetry from Greek to Latin. As the first modern scientist to provide an accurate portrayal of the universe with mathematical data rather than divine suppositions, Copernicus became one of the founding fathers of the Scientific Revolution that would alter both the cultural and religious course of Western Europe. What is primarily overlooked regarding Copernicus is his great impact on philosophy resulting from his astronomical observations. Introspection about such inarguable certainties helped displace man from the center of the universe leading future scholars and thinkers of all fields to further question accepted church doctrine.

158

12

FLAVIUS VALERIUS AURELIUS CONSTANTINUS

Christianity is currently the dominant religion with regards to followers today. It has been assumed that since the death, or even the birth of Jesus of Nazareth, that Christianity became a major religious force in the world. This is decidedly untrue. Christians were a small sect, and often persecuted by the Roman pagans. Their numbers continued to grow but one singular event sealed the religion's rise toward eventual religious supremacy. The emperor responsible for the introduction of Christianity to the Roman Empire was born on February 27th, 280 A.D in Naissus, modern day Serbia. His father became Emperor Constantius I, ruling over the Western faction of the divided Roman Empire, and his mother was later canonized as St. Helena. Flavius grew up in the court of the Emperor Diocletian, who grew weary of civil unrest and war, so he abdicated the throne in 305. Constantius was made Emperor, but died the following year. As a result of this untimely death Flavius was crowned Emperor of the West by his troops, taking the name Constantine I.

Alternate claims to the Western throne initiated another series of civil wars, which ended in 312. This victory ended any claim to the Western Roman Emperorship, with Constantine defeating all who opposed him. During the final civil battle Constantine allegedly saw a flaming cross in the sky directing him to conquer all forces opposing him. Constantine immediately converted to Christianity. The following year Constantine met with the Eastern Roman Emperor Licinius and as a result of this meeting came the Edict of Milan. The edict ended the persecution of Christians, establishing a policy of religious freedom. Within the scope of the edict all confiscated properties were to be returned to Christians, which instituted Christianity as a legitimate religion alongside paganism. Immediate effects saw the end of paganism as the official religion of the Roman Empire.

Battles over common Roman provinces continued. Constantine eventually took sole control over the entirety of the Roman Empire in 323. It was at this stage, with Constantine as sole Emperor, that Christianity became the official religion. This change was solidified in 325 during the Council of Nicaea. Constantine invited all the Christian bishops to air their grievances, whereupon legend has it that Constantine was handed the bishops grievances and burned all of them without even reading them. Conflicting doctrines would no longer be accepted within the empire and the Nicene Creed established the accepted Christian Church doctrine. This meeting was the first to bring together all of the various Christian Churches originating the marriage between Church and State that would last into the Middle Ages, and to some extent into the current world of today.

One of the most important projects Constantine completed was the relocation of the capitol from Rome to Byzantium. Constantine knew the dilemma of having the capitol situated so far from invading barbarian hordes, and therefore chose Byzantium due to its centralized position for protection of the empire's provinces and availability of an established trade route. He would rename it Constantinople. A plan of reconstruction was undertaken as Constantinople was rebuilt and expanded into one of the world's greatest cities becoming a center for thought and culture. Despite the eventual division of the Roman Empire after Constantine's death in 337 and the fall of the Western Roman Empire in 410, Constantinople remained as the capitol of the Eastern Roman Empire until 1453 when it was captured by the Ottoman Turks and renamed Istanbul.

Constantine's conversion to Christianity has been challenged and debated over the years. A comparison to Christian proselytizer St. Paul's immaculate conversion has been offered. Disputes arose however, mainly due to the continuing wars against Licinius over common provinces, the supreme rule of the empire, as well as the ambiguity surrounding having his wife and son put to death in 326. His efforts to allow for the toleration of and advancement of the burgeoning sect of Christianity should override any argument on the subject of his true religion. In addition to his religious reforms and strategic relocations Constantine was influential in his legislative acts. A decree made by Constantine forbade farmers from departing from their land, predating yet perhaps initiating the medieval practice of serfdom, which would play a distinct role in both the initial decline and eventual rise of Eastern Europe during the Middle Ages. The legacy of Constantine the Great shall remain chiefly as the first Christian Roman Emperor, yet his cultural, economic and legislative policies helped change the course of European and Middle Eastern history forever.

11

MOHAMMED

The people of the Middle East were a mixture of many cultural backgrounds and a wide variety of religious affiliations. This diversity often prompted battle and war over whose faith had authentic territorial claims. The introduction of new faiths only increased fighting, yet one faith would gather continual momentum, Islam, currently the second most widely followed religion in the world. Its founder, Mohammed, is singularly responsible for creating its entire belief structure and authoring the religion's primary text guiding daily life. Born in 570 A.D., in Mecca, present day Saudi Arabia, Mohammed's father passed away just prior to his birth and his mother died when he was only six. From that point on he was raised by his grandfather and uncle Abu Taleb, who brought Mohammed along with him during his travels throughout the Middle East. A legend has endured that Mohammed was illiterate, yet considering the impact he had upon the lives of his followers it appears that this alleged illiteracy is nothing more than embellishment to further myth.

At the age of 23, Mohammed married a wealthy widow, Khadijah, who bore him six children, two boys and four girls, five of them whom Mohammed outlived. It was at this time that Mohammed began his work as a merchant trader, bringing him into further contact with numerously diverse people, including those of both Judeo and Christian backgrounds. Their monotheistic religious belief system greatly influenced Mohammed. In 610 A.D., at the age of forty, Mohammed believed God visited him, through the archangel Gabriel. While meditating in a cave Mohammed was told that he was the messenger of Allah, the one true God, and soon thereafter began converting people into the Islamic faith. The meetings of these early converts were held in secret until a second message was revealed to Mohammed in around 614 A.D. Thereafter Mohammed openly preached the new faith, the teachings of which would be written down by his followers in the primary text of the religion, the *Koran*. Over the next couple of years, the persecution of Muslims began, eventually forcing Mohammed to flee Mecca for his own safety.

In 620 A.D., pilgrims from Medina, a small city to the north of Mecca, heard Mohammed's preaching. Medina was primarily a monotheistic region that, after hearing Mohammed preach, became convinced Mohammed was the prophet anticipated in Hebrew folklore. The following year a large group of Medinese returned to Mecca and adopted Islam as their religion, offering Mohammed the political power he would need to spread his message, albeit within the city of Medina. In 622 A.D., called the *Hegira*, or year of the flight, Mohammed fled Mecca for his own safety and immigrated to Medina. The agreement between Mohammed and the Medinese was that Mohammed's loyal followers would be allowed to follow him to Medina, which was gladly accepted by the Medinese. Within Medina the population became overwhelmingly Islamic due to the presence of Mohammed and his teachings. Over the next seven years there were vicious wars ending with Mohammed claiming a final victory in 630 A.D., making Mecca a Muslim site for holy pilgrimages.

By the time of his death in 632 A.D., Mohammed had married six more times, after the death of his first wife, yet none of them bore him a male heir. More importantly he had converted a large number of Arab tribes and clans over to Islam and united these previously warring groups into one cohesive force, which would eventually transform the scope of Western history through their conquests and battles. Although seen principally as a religious figure Mohammed became the complete and sole ruler of the Arabian peninsula in a relatively short period of time. With a platform of power Mohammed was virtually unabated in spreading his new faith. Despite the purity of his heart in purveying a message of religious importance, the manner in which it was carried out was brutality and war. This continued with the followers of Mohammed, who by 711 A.D. had amassed the largest empire the world had known, converting their captives to the Islamic faith. Originally started as God's work, Islamic fundamentalism has become synonymous with terror, although that is seen predominantly through European Christian eyes. Mohammed was unique among key religious figures as he both actively participated in converting citizens and authored the ethical values that became the guiding philosophy behind Islam. It is a shame that religious freedom becomes synonymous with War, a standard that an inherently pacifistic Mohammed, whose greatness shall always be clouded, had to come to terms with and ultimately succumb to its harsh reality.

10

ARCHIMEDES

The Golden Age of Greece, just prior to Rome's emergence as a superpower, produced a wealth of pioneering knowledge unmatched by any other previous or succeeding period. Establishing the basic principles of every major field of knowledge, this era, consisting of not only Greek scholars, guided man toward the advancement of knowledge. One particular field was mathematics, and a Sicilian named Archimedes raised that advancement to a higher level than ever achieved before. Born in 287 B.C. in Syracuse, on the island of Sicily, his father, Phidias, was a renowned astronomer and Archimedes followed in his footsteps, studying mathematics and science in Alexandria, Egypt. After his education in Alexandria, Archimedes returned to Syracuse where he would live and work for the remainder of his life. Extremely little is known of Archimedes' personal life. No records or written information on Archimedes marrying or having children have survived, so his mathematical theorems and mechanical inventions remain as his legacy.

The specified field of mathematics that interested Archimedes was geometry, developing formulas for obtaining the volume and surface area of a sphere. Additional theorems and formulas applied to circles, cylinders, planes and cones, all necessary components of geometric mathematics. So passionate about geometry was Archimedes that he described his mechanical inventions as 'geometry at play'. In these analyses Archimedes came extremely close to inventing calculus. What Archimedes did invent were forms of integral and differential calculus within the framework of his problem solving. His formula for the relationship between a sphere and a cylinder was considered by Archimedes to be his own greatest achievement, instructing that it was to be marked upon his grave. Archimedes' practical theorems and developed mathematical clarifications of previously known geometric principles advanced the study of geometry into an applied science. Recent research has unearthed that some of his work also laid the basic groundwork for trigonometry.

In one of Archimedes' landmark works he explored the concept of gravity and demonstrably proved the law of the lever, known as the law of simple machines. The legendary anecdotal record of his research regarding the lever was that if he were given a place to stand he could move the Earth. When challenged, Archimedes single handedly dragged a full barge ashore using a compound pulley, known today as a block and tackle, which he invented for this specific demonstration. Although geometry was Archimedes passion he invented a number of operational devices that advanced science and aided in both the protection and cultural development of his home. His endless screw was a spiral pipe that raised water in an uphill motion. Its practical applications relate to irrigation and the pumping of water. Another device was an orrery, which accurately described the motion of the planets, moon and the sun. Archimedes was able to build and operate a catapult to launch objects from land onto invading ships, thereby establishing an early form of ballistics.

The most definitive scientific principle attributed to Archimedes bears his name, also known as buoyancy. When he was asked to determine the purity of a gold crown Archimedes established the property of density through the volume of water displacement. This became the fundamental principle in the field of hydrostatics, of which Archimedes is generally acknowledged as the founder of. The implications of his principle of buoyancy led Archimedes to develop the concept of equilibrium. This concept's practical application translated into building larger and heavier ships that would not capsize, increasing trade and aiding naval efficiency.

Whether or not the anecdotal stories of Archimedes' exploits were that of fact or fiction, they undoubtedly kept alive the records of his laborious efforts into establishing a clearer understanding of mathematics. His work with the lever, pulley and screw created the fundamental work in the field of physics. There is not a mathematically related field that Archimedes did not discover major original principles, help to advance, or purely establish. His achievements in these areas are of paramount importance and his death in 212 B.C. by the invading Roman army was the simple mistake of a foot soldier. Upon his death at the age of seventy-five, Archimedes was still applying his mathematical genius to practical inventions. It is difficult to estimate what Archimedes might have created during his final days had he not been accidentally killed. Perhaps everything?

9

CHARLES DARWIN

The differing fields of science re-emerged during the 16th century, continuing and flourishing through the 17th and 18th centuries. Amazing scientific discoveries were hypothesized and revealed to the scientific community, who would in turn provide these breakthroughs to the world. Scientific progress continued into the 19th century, when the world would be provided with such a remarkably ground breaking theory, by Charles Darwin, that would explode the legend of creationism, sending shockwaves throughout both the biological and religious communities. Born on February 12th, 1809 in Shrewsbury, England, Darwin's father sent Charles to a private school in Shrewsbury. The young Charles was not an attentive student. The programs of study were not to his liking, however he was a keen observer and collected various animals and plant samples, foreshadowing his future career as a naturalist. At sixteen, Darwin enrolled at Edinburgh University in Scotland, with the goal of studying medicine. He would soon become bored and annoyed with this course of study.

After leaving his medical studies behind, Darwin was persuaded to begin studying for the clergy. In 1828 he entered Christ's Church in Cambridge and wasted no time in neglecting his clerical studies in favor of natural history and biology. Befriended by two natural history professors, Darwin was invited to join the research vessel, the *H.M.S. Beagle* on its five-year voyage to the South Seas. After some convincing Darwin's father allowed Charles to accept the invitation, as an unpaid naturalist, and the ship set sail on December 27th, 1831. His knack for collecting was apparent as Charles gathered information and data on everything he saw during the entirety of the voyage. When the ship returned to England on October 2nd, 1836 Darwin had gathered more than enough information to begin formulating his legendary theory. One minor detail was missing from the puzzle, which Darwin would discover in 1838.

While reading the 1798 essay on population by Malthus, Darwin would discover the missing component, fashioning his theory of natural selection. Natural selection states that individuals with genetic compositions suited for survival will rise above and succeed over those whose genetic characteristics and predispositions are not as profound, the elementary basis for Darwin's survival of the fittest. Darwin continued to collect and analyze data over the next twenty years, never publishing his theory until fate stepped in during 1858. Independent of Darwin's research fellow British naturalist Alfred Russel Wallace forwarded Darwin his own research to obtain his opinion. Their research was almost identical, prompting Darwin to present an outline for his book and Wallace's findings to a zoological society. While the 1858 presentations did not receive critical success, the following year Darwin released his landmark book *On the Origin of Species.*

Darwin's 1859 book was an immediate success, causing a sensation unseen before and his reputation was immediately cemented in both the field of biology and natural philosophy, due to the implications of his evolutionary theories. Twelve years later Darwin would produce *The Descent of Man,* which put forth the groundbreaking theory that man descending from a lower order of ape-like primates, adding additional controversy in the world of theology. Darwin wrote on the subject of natural selection until he passed away, on April 19th, 1882. Much has been made of his personal lack of defense of his theory of evolution, yet since returning from the South Seas he had become sickly and spent the bulk remainder of his life researching and writing the basic tenets of his theory.

Darwin's primary importance occurs from his own lack of knowledge regarding genetics, which compliments his theory so perfectly. Similar to the empirical scientists before him Darwin supplied the data and evidentiary research to substantiate natural selection, placing it on an equal level as the natural laws discovered regarding the cosmos. The impact of Darwin's work reaches far beyond the scope of biology. Darwinism has also become a major element in the social scientific fields of anthropology and sociology. To this day, almost 150 years after the original publication of his book, no scientist or theologian has been able to positively refute Darwin's theory. Darwin's theory can be narrowed down to one word, hope. The hope that humans might one day understand we may not be the immaculate creatures above all others, resulting from Darwin's research, may one day lead towards altruistic cooperation and peace. Perhaps his theory's longest lasting impression may occur in the way us humans ultimately view each other, as evolutionary equals.

8

GALILEO GALILEI

Science became modernized in the 16th century, yet in the annals of modern science Galileo Galilei holds a distinct place in history. His contributions extend to numerous branches of science and have paved the way for future researchers to expand upon his formulas and empirical research. Born on February 15th, 1564 in the town of Pisa, Italy, Galileo originally studied medicine after leaving a Jesuit monastery at an early age. Medicine held no particular interest and in turn Galileo turned to mathematics. Without a degree or a completed formal education, Galileo had obtained a teaching position in Florence and would go onto invent his first noteworthy mechanism, a geometric compass, which calculated a comparison of proportional triangles.

Prior to teaching in Florence and eventually Padua, Galileo, only seventeen years old, discovered the theory of specific gravity involving the movements of a pendulum. This discovery, usually not associated with Galileo, led to the development of the pendulum clock. While teaching mathematics in Padua, Galileo experimented with mechanics and hydrostatics and in 1594 Galileo obtained a patent for a machine that raised underground water. Galileo's machine was essential for land irrigation advancing the concept created by Archimedes eighteen centuries earlier. Galileo himself constructed a thermoscope, a predecessor of the thermometer in the field of thermodynamics, which was able to measure minor changes in pressure.

During this early period of discovery and invention Galileo's two most important breakthroughs were establishing a uniformed rate of acceleration and the law of inertia. Influenced by early proponents of ballistics, Galileo challenged a long-standing belief held by the Greek philosopher Aristotle, heavier objects fall faster than lighter objects. Not only was Galileo able to disprove this belief, he summarized his empirical data in a concise mathematical formula. Galileo's law of inertia is stated as, an object shall retain both its velocity and direction unless acted upon by an outside force to alter or halt that direction. As gravity remains a constant factor, a downward infinite continuance is not possible, yet Galileo theorized that a ball rolling along the ground would continue rolling until it was met by an outside force. This law is the foundation for modern physics, while his mathematical deductions based on experimental data regarding rate of acceleration and curvature rate of descent helped to establish modern scientific methodology.

In 1609 Galileo heard of the construction of a telescope and without actually seeing the device was able to construct a far superior model. Galileo discovered that the sun rotates on its own axis due to the periodic observation of sunspots. He observed four bodies that he determined to be moons revolving around Jupiter, becoming the first to cite them. This implied that satellites could rotate around planets other than the Earth indicating that the Earth was not the center of the universe. His most vital discovery was that the planet Venus displayed distinct phases, implying that these variations in appearance were a direct result of the illumination of the Sun; in effect proving the heliocentric model of the universe propounded by Copernicus. Upon this discovery and Galileo's subsequent writings and teachings of heliocentric cosmology, the Church immediately stepped in and attempted to censor this progressive thinker, despite overwhelming mathematical evidence.

Galileo's conflicts with the Church over the censorship of his theories are of legendary status. Decrees were passed outlawing such theories, yet Galileo continued writing and expounding his accurate knowledge of the universe. Eventually the Church would win as Galileo was condemned and exiled. By 1638 Galileo had gone blind by observing sunspots and he would pass away in 1642 in his villa at Arcetri, Italy. Despite recanting his views on heliocentric cosmology to appease the Church in order to save his life, three hundred and fifty years later, in an overt act of public relations, the Roman Catholic Church admitted that Galileo was unfairly condemned, exiled and censored regarding his astronomical theories. That stolen portion of Galileo's life, which was evidently devoted to astronomy, can never be repaid. We can only imagine what other fascinating discoveries may have arisen. Notwithstanding the powerful impact of Galileo's works in the field of thermodynamics, hydrostatics, mechanics, ballistics, physics, mathematics and the establishment of modern scientific methodology, Galileo shall always be remembered for his pioneering work in astronomy and the resulting struggles he faced to simply reveal the truth.

JESUS OF NAZARETH

If this were a book solely based on the influence any individual would have had upon history then the 1st century Jewish prophet would certainly top the list. This however, examines significance, a blend of both influence and importance, which as a result lowers the actual placing of this immensely historic figure. The life of Jesus that is historically known is the fewest of any person on this list, mentioned before or the six to come. Historians only know of twelve years of this man's life, although the final four and first one, provide the legend that has turned Jesus from preacher to messiah, from man to perfect deity, unchallengeable and revered by those who follow him. Jesus was born in Bethlehem, in Roman Palestine during 4 B.C. A more likely date for his birth would be December 25th, 5 B.C. 4 B.C. has become the general established date, yet the above dilemma remains when December 25th is designated as the birthday of Jesus. The year 5 B.C. did hold astrological significance; most likely prompting the wandering of the three wise men in search of an otherworldly being, yet that debate is for another time. For now 4, or late 5 B.C., is enough to go by.

The New Testament of the Holy Bible is the only record of this man's life. What is even more baffling is that nothing was written about Jesus during his lifetime. The books dedicated to the life of Jesus were not written until at least a minimum of 30 years after Jesus was put to death, with some written over 70 years after. While oral tradition may be used as a source of information, it is not always wholly accurate, while also having been written by men who had never actually met Jesus, yet rather received their information from others who passed it down through the years. By that time a legend had been grown regarding Jesus, yet along those lines it seems incredibly strange that no other record of this man exists, or at least has been found to this date. One would think that a man performing such prodigious miracles would have been recorded among the history of a land with numerous cultures, which included Roman, Jewish and Arab. That did not occur.

His teachings, what Jesus is revered for, were of high moral codes emphasizing honesty, patience, tolerance and modesty. These ideals form the basis of Christianity, which evolved years after the actual life and death of Jesus.

Through his instruction he began to gather a following. This angered the religious leaders of the day, most notably the leaders within Judaism. It may have been a disapproval of Jesus' teaching methods that got him arrested and eventually crucified. While his ideas were not entirely original, having their basis within Eastern philosophy, it is highly unlikely that Jesus knew they pre-existed. Yet perhaps those missing years of Jesus' life were spent traveling the world, where he came in contact such with Eastern philosophies. His attempt to teach Eastern philosophical religion seriously deviated from the standard religious teaching practices of the day. Whatever it was that caused Jesus' death sentence, his ideas live on, yet unfortunately are not practiced universally. That fact, while not affecting his highly influential stature, seriously diminishes the significance of Jesus.

What must be understood about this entry is that the mythic figure Christ is not included on this list. Christ is a deity, and without entering into a long and impossible to resolve debate, a deity is different from an individual. Jesus of Nazareth was a man. It is that man who has been placed on this list. The immediate argument that will arise is that to say Jesus was a man is blasphemy, yet when asked to explain the mysteries and comparative misstatements regarding Jesus' life no legitimate answer is given. Faith is offered, yet this is a work of non-fiction history. Mere faith has no place within historical data, and this concept needs to be understood. His ideals, while utopian, would indeed make the world a better place, seriously increasing his significance, yet the almost total ignoring or manipulating of those ideals does reduce his overall rank. The simple fact that the only historical record of Jesus not only contradicts itself when cross-referenced, but was also not written during his lifetime, calls the validity of those records into question. No one can challenge that Jesus has had a deep impact upon history, perhaps deeper than any man on this list, yet the unfortunate reality must be dealt with, the legend of his life was created years after his death. On sheer ideology Jesus belongs among the top tier of this list. I just wish more would take his true principles to heart, rather than maneuvering them for one's own individual benefit. Jesus was not about the individual, but rather about the world as a whole. With such lofty standards, it baffles the mind as to why they need continual re-interpretation.

SAUL OF TARSUS

With any new religion a specific set of rules must be established. The teachings of a wandering prophet alone are not merely enough to sustain faith and convert followers. Sometimes those who institute guidelines are far more vital to those who merely preach ideas, none more so than in the case of St. Paul. Originally one of the chief detractors of Jesus, known as Saul, he became the earliest proselytizer of the Christian faith. Born in 4 A.D., at Tarsus in Cilicia, present-day Turkey, Saul was of Hebrew descent brought up as a Roman citizen. His education was multicultural consisting primarily within the framework of the Jewish tradition, yet he was an ardent student of philosophy, eventually learning tent making as a formal trade. After traveling to Jerusalem, Saul became an passionate opposer to the burgeoning sect of Christians and took an active part in Christian persecution. Sometime around 40 A.D. Saul claims to have encountered a vision that would dramatically alter his worldly perception, setting the course of his life on a strange new path.

As recorded in the New Testament, Saul was struck down and blinded by a vision of Jesus Christ, who spoke to him. Saul immediately converted to Christianity and his sight was later restored. He changed his name to Paul and began to preach the teachings of Jesus. Saul met with Jesus' disciples to formulate a plan, spreading Jesus' message. A ten-year missionary journey throughout the Mediterranean began, where Christian churches were established and a multitude of converts were made. At some time around 60 A.D. Paul traveled to Jerusalem where he was arrested for preaching Christianity. He spent approximately two years in jail in Jerusalem, eventually making his way to Rome after his release. When Paul reached Rome the minor Christian community embraced him. Paul was arrested and later executed by the Roman Emperor Nero, around 67 A.D.

The Bible is known for its long-standing mythology regarding divinity, creationism and the lineage of the original men, so it is increasingly hard to separate fact from folklore. What is not in question, yet decidedly overlooked, is that Paul is responsible for at least fourteen of the twenty-seven books of the New Testament, the official manual governing Christian life. Paul was a master letter writer, and contained within these letters, the whole basis of Christian doctrine is laid out. Paul is responsible for numerous accepted principles within Christian theology including the pure divinity of Jesus (Christ), the second coming of the messiah (Christ) who died for the sins of humans, supremacy of Christian dogma over Mosaic / Hebrew law, the spiritual regeneration through accepting Christ, the concept of original sin and a general wholehearted acceptance of the teachings of Christ to guide daily life. These messages imply that faith alone shall lead toward eternal salvation, placing what was a minor sect into a unified religion with an established organizational system.

Paul was one of the outspoken leaders against the equal rights of women. It has never been determined if Paul married and a school of thought exists that he may have lived a life of celibacy, derived from his writings where he encourages celibacy or sex within marriage only. In this Paul considered sex outside the sanctity of marriage a sin punishable by death, yet made no reward for accepting Christ to nullify these sins, displaying his supreme disregard for the opposite sex and the evil nature of women. There are distinct differences in the teachings of Jesus and the writings of Paul, yet the uncompromising acceptance of Paul's writings as the authority of Christian doctrine helped suppress women for close to two thousand years. While other societies embraced women, Christians remained in the Dark Ages, treating their life partners as servants rather than equals.

This is not the forum to discuss the divinity described by Saul regarding Jesus and his teachings, yet rather to analyze the importance Saul played in world events. Through Saul's writing however, one can ponder the question; did Saul create Christ, as he provided the corresponding theological dogma necessary to perpetuate the message of Jesus? Through his missionary work the sect of Christianity blossomed and although persecution continued, Christianity would be embraced, becoming the official religion of the Roman Empire under Constantine in 325. Saul has often been considered the most influential figure in Christianity after Jesus, although that is somewhat erroneous. Saul is the without a doubt the most important figure in Christian history, not only founding the principles its based upon, but also establishing its folklore and spreading its initial message throughout the world.

ISAAC NEWTON

Prior to the 17th century science, physics in particular, was a mixture of theory and religion. It was increasingly hard to wrest established science from the church without concise integrated information that could be proved mathematically. Galileo made the first step but the work of Isaac Newton ensured that science would no longer be administered by church doctrine, but by mathematical certainty. Born on December 25th, 1642, in Woolsthorpe, England, during his early schooling Newton appeared distracted at times, so he was removed from school as a teenager. Newton tried his hand at becoming a farmer, but at the age of eighteen Newton was sent to study at Cambridge University, focusing on mathematics and science. In 1664 Newton was allowed to execute his own independent research at Trinity College, and prior to leaving school due to its closure from an outbreak of the plague, Newton discovered the binomial theorem. The discoveries Newton made while on leave from school however, prior to the age of twenty-five, would revolutionize the world as it was currently known.

Newton's first breakthrough was in mathematics, the invention of differential calculus. Calculus is the branch of mathematics that dealt with variable quantities, including the movement of bodies and waves. Calculus is required in the solving of all problems relating to physical movement. Through the advent of calculus, Newton was able to mathematically display how his fundamental laws of mechanics were applicable to solving actual material problems, used throughout his 1687 masterpiece to show precise calculations of astronomical observations. Considered to be the greatest mathematical development in the modern scientific era, it became indispensable for the expansion of modern mathematical theory.

His second major discovery occurred in the field of optics beginning from his formulation of the law of composition of light, also known as the corpuscular theory of light. Newton observed that light was a stream of non-interacting particles, prompting Newton to analyze the nature of color, specifically the character of the white light of the Sun. Using a prism, white light was shown to be a mixture of rays of light combining all the colors of the visible spectrum. Using previously discovered laws of refraction and reflection of light, combined with his own theory, Newton was able to build the first workable reflecting telescope allowing man to significantly advance astronomical observation.

The third, and perhaps most vital discovery was the law of universal gravitation, where objects experienced a gravitational force proportional to the inverse square of the distance separating them, while also proportional to the product of their specific masses. As a result Newton was able to positively state and prove the moon was directed around the Earth, as well as the planets around the Sun accounting for their elliptical orbits, by the mere force of gravitation. Gravity was therefore responsible for balancing the centrifugal force of the planets, illustrating the Earth was not a perfect sphere, but slightly flattened at the poles. Gravity was also shown by Newton to affect the tides, related to its impact on the Moon and the Sun.

In 1687, Newton published the landmark work in modern science, *Mathematical Principles of Natural Philosophy*. Within it are described Newton's three laws of motion, inertia, motion and reaction, the second of which, the law of motion, is the central law of conventional physics. Combining these laws with the universal law of gravitation Newton was able to explain that his theory was universally applicable, yet more importantly express these statements in precise mathematical form to verify his theory. The *Principia*, as it is more commonly known, would establish hydrodynamics, hydrostatics and mathematical physics, launching them into the realm of modern applied sciences. By combining numerous fields and variously developed laws and theorems, Newton was able to construct a unified system, where previously, a hypothetical world existed. Newton's system could both solve unexplainable occurrences and devise predictions mathematically. These mathematical certainties led to an explosion of applicable astronomical data relating to the solar system, which had eluded scientists, who hypothesized that it could not be obtained. Isaac Newton believed the nature of science was to explore the boundaries of knowledge and learning in an attempt to understand the true nature of being. His death in 1727 unfortunately ended that journey of discovery.

AMENHOTEP IV

The concept of monotheism, a belief in one singular God is practiced by roughly ninety-nine percent of those holding religious beliefs. This principle seems as common today as polytheism, belief in many Gods, was in ancient times. This is not to state that all of mankind believes in the same God, and numerous wars occur to disprove that axiom. The original idea of monotheism has been attributed to the Persian prophet Zoroaster and or the Biblical Jewish patriarch Abraham, although it is increasingly hard to separate myth from history. From an historical standpoint monotheism may have been first conceived in the 14th century B.C., by an Egyptian pharaoh, named Amenhotep IV. Amenhotep IV took over as ruler of the Eighteenth Dynasty in approximately 1378 B.C. It is generally agreed upon that Amenhotep IV began his reign as a teenager, which should approximate the date of his birth at around 1395 B.C. The second son of Amenhotep III and Tiye, Amenhotep IV inherited an empire that had amassed a wealth of foreign lands throughout Asia.

During the early years of his reign, Amenhotep IV was aided in his Royal affairs by his mother, and then by his wife Nefertiti. Prior to the sixth year of his sovereignty, Amenhotep IV changed his name and began enforcing his monotheistic belief system within the empire. Early in his reign as pharaoh, Amenhotep IV changed his name to Akhenaten, translated as, 'one who is useful to Aten'. Aten was the God of the Sun. Immediately Amenhotep IV denied the divinity of all other Gods and undertook a large-scale project, abandoning the long time Egyptian capitol city of Thebes to construct an entirely new uninhabited city, dedicated to Aten. This new city, located in the center of Egypt surrounded by cliffs that bear a striking resemblance to the horizon, was called Akhetaten, currently known as el-Amarna. This move was indicative of Amenhotep's break with the past, diverting away from the prior polytheistic belief system to impose his own ideal of a singular God, Aten. Amenhotep's religious beliefs were so rigid and self-engrossing that the foreign affairs of the empire were allowed to lapse causing dissention and ultimately rebellion within Egypt's dominion.

The artistic culture of Egypt flourished during the time of Amenhotep IV, shifting from the prior Egyptian style of ideal features. These designs were replaced with a more realistic approach, emphasizing the individual's uniqueness with religious overtones, again done with respect to Aten. Amenhotep IV had a penchant for celebrations and numerous festivals are recorded to display respect to Aten and reinforce his divinity as sovereign King. Temples were constructed and a large quarry project was undertaken, yet imposed taxes on these and similar building ventures, coupled with the priests from the previous era disapproving of his denouncement of the old Gods, made Amenhotep IV extremely unpopular among his subjects.

The idea of one God evolved over time and was not initially accepted, as is indicated by the immediate return to the polytheistic practices by the succeeding pharaoh. The practice of selective monotheism can be directly attributable to a large percentage of the bloodiest wars in recorded history, however the principle of one God has also shaped the course of history so drastically that polytheism and atheism are generally rejected as acceptable belief systems. That same persecution that excluded the early advancement of monotheism now halts the return of polytheism or the rejection of theism in favor of science. Although the right to freedom of religion should be afforded to all, an abuse of this concept negates any positive benefits of allowing such a freedom.

One must wonder if Amenhotep IV's advent of monotheism, albeit an advancement in thought, actually had a positive effect on civilization? Perhaps monotheism was merely intended as a selfish endeavor on the part of Amenhotep IV to secure a place in history and in the afterlife? Amenhotep IV also may have launched the first civil service, yet given his religious propensity it seems that any such undertaking would have dealt specifically with the honoring of Aten, rather than a pure benefit to the common Egyptian people. By the time of his death, between 1350 and 1338 B.C., he was so unpopular, from a combination of revolutionary religious practices and the declining status of the empire that an immediate return to the past commenced. An advancer of contrary thought such as Amenhotep IV, whether it is scientific or religious, generally endures dissent from those who fear change, yet they shall always remain as the true innovators within society.

194

3

JOHANN GENSFLEISCH

Printing originated in China, perhaps as far back as the 6th century A.D. using the slow and time-consuming wood block method. It is widely accepted that a Chinese alchemist, who used a mixture of clay and glue hardened by baking, invented movable type printing in 1041. An improvement to this process was made by an agriculturalist, who used movable wooden blocks at the end of the 13th century. Metal type printing was used in Korea prior to the mid 15th century, with research and development funded by the government. Western printing may be traced to 1423, when metal characters were used to print the Roman alphabet, creating a clay printing plate. However, it was a German businessman named Johann Gensfleisch who would advance the field of printing into the annals of history with an invention that would maximize the full potential of the written word. This critical invention set the stage for an entire revolution in thought throughout Europe.

Johann Gensfleisch was born in approximately 1398, in Mainz, Germany, later adopting his mother's maiden name of Gutenberg, for business purposes. Extremely little is known about Gutenberg's early life. He moved to Strasbourg, which currently lies in France, in about 1428 and spent the next 20 or so years there. A legal record documents this as fact, the last official documentation occurring in 1444. Prior to originally moving to Strasbourg there is speculation that he developed his talent for working with metals as an ironworker. Other sources allege that Gutenberg honed his skill working as a goldsmith, but there is evidence that a working partnership was entered into by Gutenberg to produce metal hand mirrors, which were used in religious pilgrimages and ceremonies. By the time Gutenberg returned to Mainz, in 1448, he was on his way to developing the printing press, with the idea of increasing printing productivity formalized within him.

Gutenberg began his printing endeavors in Strasbourg, probably around 1436. The loan on record to Gutenberg in 1448, the earliest documentation of his return to Mainz, could easily be explained as covering the setting up of a workshop. Two loans were given to Gutenberg from a goldsmith named Johann Fust. As collateral, Gutenberg's printing equipment was signed over to Fust. Gutenberg produced multiple editions of a Latin grammar book and a Latin dictionary. Growing weary of waiting for repayment, a legal battle ensued and Fust took over the shop and equipment that housed Gutenberg's printing press. Fust, with the help of a technician who had worked for Gutenberg, became the leading printers in Mainz. Their success was created using Gutenberg's press, which Fust now legally owned. The famous 1455 Bible, in German, attributed to Gutenberg, may have been completed after he lost possession of his shop and equipment. It was Gutenberg's dream however, and hard work that made the printing press a reality. His method for improved printing, creating a complete and efficient printing technique that was capable of mass production, allowed others to stake their claim as premier printers, while Gutenberg received little or no money from his revolutionary creation.

Gutenberg's dynamic improvements on the Chinese movable type method of printing had an astounding effect on European society. The Protestant Reformation of 1517 is a perfect example; two prior attempts at a Protestant Reformation had failed because they were mainly localized, and thus easily thwarted by the mighty arm of the Catholic Church. Directly because of the mass production capability of Gutenberg's printing press, Luther's 1517 reformation was able to reach a wide variety and mass of people from numerous areas. This ensured that the Church could not suppress Luther's message as it had done twice before, thus altering the course of European as well as both North and South American cultural history. The exact same formula can be utilized to explain the immediate impact that the Scientific Revolution had upon Europe and the rest of the world. Gutenberg's printing press allowed for books and manuscripts, which had been costly to produce and therefore reserved for nobility and the social elite, to become readily available to the general public. As a result an educated middle-class developed within Europe, who would come to challenge established doctrine rather than having to accept policy as fact. Johann Gutenberg continued printing after losing his press in 1455, until blindness forced him to retire, later passing away on February 3rd, 1468. He died without the knowledge of how enormous his invention would actually impact the world.

2

LOUIS PASTEUR

Despite numerous medical innovations after the end of the Middle Ages, medicine still remained somewhat of a mystical science. Death, as a result of infection and disease, was often merely accepted within the medical profession as an unfortunate side effect of the harshness of life. The Industrial Revolution did not benefit mankind, specifically relating to health, with new medical problems arising. Certain men of science would not continue along the path of mere acceptance. As a result the life expectancy of humans has increased, directly attributable to the advances made in science and medicine. At the forefront of these medical and scientific breakthroughs was Louis Pasteur. Born on December 27th, 1822, in Dole, France, Pasteur did not excel during his early education, focusing on artistic endeavors such as painting. An aptitude for chemistry led Pasteur to continue his formal education in France, training directly toward a career in science.

While working toward a Doctorate in Chemistry in 1848 Pasteur investigated the newly emerging branch of chemistry known as Crystallography. Pasteur began work on crystals formed from tartaric acids, which appeared to have similar chemical compounds, yet demonstrated differing optical properties. He discovered that isomers of the same crystal were mirror images of each other, discovering an entirely new class of substances, dissymmetric molecules. Pasteur established a fundamental law; asymmetry differentiates the organic world from the mineral world, correctly declaring that asymmetrical molecules were indicative of living processes. Pasteur's work on molecular asymmetry founded a new science, stereochemistry, which has major practical applications in current day pharmacological research.

Pasteur later examined the process of alcohol fermentation and the long-standing notion of spontaneous generation. Fermentation of alcohol from sugar was believed to be a chemical process yet Pasteur discovered that it was a biological process. Yeast, a living organism, was thought to be a necessary byproduct of fermentation. Pasteur proved that yeast was actually responsible for the fermentation process and that contamination occurred from specific microorganisms. Spontaneous generation argues that life could arise spontaneously in organic materials. Pasteur disproved this, by demonstrating microorganisms were contained within air. Pasteur's disproval of spontaneous generation evolved into his germ theory of disease, which became one of the most important medical breakthroughs in history. He isolated specific microorganisms, resulting in his process of using heat to eradicate contaminated microorganisms, sterilizing fermentation batches. This process is known as Pasteurization, and is widely used today. These insights are the foundation of microbiology.

His main contribution to humankind occurred in the field of immunology. Discovering the method for the reduction of virulent microorganisms, which compromises the basis of vaccination; Pasteur isolated the organism responsible for producing cholera in chicken. After successful attempts at inoculation of infected fowl, Pasteur acknowledged a general principle of vaccination; isolate the specific microbe and inject a reduced potency to produce immunity. He then turned his efforts to attacking anthrax, which can be spread to humans, and produced a vaccine that all but eliminated this recurrent problem. Further research on immunology concluded with an investigation into the fatal disease rabies. Pasteur was forced to test his rabies vaccine on an infected boy. When his inoculations cured the young boy the doors were opened in the medical community to battle numerous diseases that had previously been deemed fatal and without hope.

Pasteur's breadth of scientific knowledge and work ethic did not allow for failure as a possibility, resulting in a lifelong effort to improve life. Through Pasteur's work with fermentation he was able to identify anaerobic organisms, the existence of life without oxygen. His germ theory of disease led toward increased preventative measures in hospitals to minimize the spread of germs, originally proposed by Semmelweis. He helped saved the French silk industry by controlling the breeding processes of diseased silkworm eggs. His immunological work led to further developments in vaccinations to eradicate harmful diseases. Louis Pasteur passed away on September 28th, 1895, a national and worldwide hero. He is considered as a benefactor of humanity and may be singularly responsible for the advancement of life that occurred after the 19th century, resulting in his pioneering work to expand the lifespan of human beings through the advent of improved medicine.

1

ARISTOTLE

No theory, concept or notion exists until it is created. Even after their creation, specific ideas, which evolve into distinct fields, must be nurtured and eventually mastered. Mastering one field is admirable, while multiple disciplines usually earn one an honored place in the history books. During the time of the Renaissance period noted scholars amassed a considerable wealth of knowledge over a wide variety of subjects. Seventeen centuries earlier however, a Greek genius named Aristotle was the unheralded authority over a wider range of subjects than any other person, previously or since. Known today primarily as a philosopher, Aristotle was born in Stagirus, Greece in 384 B.C. His father, Nicomachus, was the court physician to the King of Macedon, yet both of his parents would pass away when he was approximately ten. An uncle or family friend of Nicomachus, Proxenus, would bring up Aristotle. At the age of seventeen Aristotle enrolled in Plato's Academy in Athens. After a short stint as a student Aristotle quickly rose to the level of instructor.

He would remain at the Academy for twenty years, before moving to Assos, an island in modern day Turkey. Politics at the time prompted Aristotle to eventually leave Assos in 342 B.C., traveling to Macedonia where he tutored the young Alexander the Great. Once Alexander came to power, Aristotle founded a rival academy in Athens in 335 B. C., called the Lyceum. It would be from this academy where the bulk of Aristotle's survived writings and commentaries on subjects originated. These writings have advanced research in every major facet of knowledge, from science to thought to even the basic improvement of average every day life. In 323 B.C., the anti-Macedonian feeling in Athens after the death of Alexander impelled Aristotle to flee Athens for Chalcis, the birthplace of his mother. The following year, Aristotle would pass away from an undisclosed stomach illness, leaving over four hundred works behind, of which approximately only one hundred and seventy remain, cataloguing all the existing knowledge of his era.

Although not the father of medicine, Aristotle is considered the founding father of biology, embryology and zoology. Aristotle's original concepts in the field of biology shaped the progress of that and related fields for centuries, with some of his postulations still remaining a mystery to the biological community today. Another topic established by Aristotle was ethics, where he attempted to ascertain man's proper role in society in an attempt to achieve happiness. Taking the work of Plato one step further, Aristotle was able to advance the philosophy of politics into political science. Perhaps no discipline within Aristotle's mastery is more important than logic. The ability to analyze a problem and arrive at a solution advanced not only thought, but also advances civilization. To formulate such a system is an achievement without equal. If logic were Aristotle's singular creation and contribution to the world that would be enough for any lifetime, yet it is his diverse breadth of knowledge encompassing numerous subjects that make him a pioneer in the field of thought.

The subjects that Aristotle can claim to have either created, excelled at, advanced or mastered are as follows: systematic, deductive and syllogistic logic, metaphysics, mathematics, zoology, biology, anatomy, astronomy, analytics, physics, rhetoric, education, theology, ethics, meteorology, politics, embryology, poetry, economics, aesthetics, democracy, medicine, hematology, oration, geography, physiology, geometry, psychology, his most known field philosophy and his most important subject matter, the advancement of knowledge and capacity for thought.

It is difficult to place Aristotle within the framework of one particular field since his writings covered all known fields. More than any other person on this list, Aristotle has changed the way daily life has evolved through the basic process of thought. He truly believed that all events, past and present, could be interpreted through analytical knowledge and logical reason, two distinct disciplines for which Aristotle can be considered the father of. He thereby created an early form of metaphysical empiricism, which would later pave the way toward provable scientific research. His rational and logical views on a wide range of subjects were admired by geniuses, censored by tyrants and despots, revived by Christian, Jewish and Islamic visionaries and generally followed by the entire scholarly world until the latter part of the 17th century, almost 2,000 years after these ideas were formed and molded. An icon before the indulgent times of the present, Aristotelian is a compliment without equal, yet worthy of no one but the genius from whom the name derives.

206

SUMMARY AND CONCLUSION

There you have it. My own subjective opinion of the 50 Most Significant Individuals in Recorded History as placed before you, the reader. Immediately most will question not only the specific rankings, yet also those notable omissions, of whom I hope you were all eagerly waiting to read about and see where they would place. It is suspense such as that which most lists lack, tending to begin with the top entry and then work its way ridiculously upwards. As far as the specific rankings, such as why was Leonardo Da Vinci ranked behind Eratosthenes or why was Solon ranked ahead of Einstein, the only answer I can add is that you will not like my answer. It is subjective, and the reasons are laid out within the text.

As far as notable omissions, a number of famous individuals were left off this list. Christopher Columbus will probably spring to mind. Columbus actually never did discover America. At least four known groups, the Chinese, the Vikings, the Phoenicians and the Native American Indians, nomadic Asiatic tribes, all reached America before Columbus. His claim to the most important modern discovery of America is erroneous, due to colonization not resulting until a suitable cash crop was discovered in the 1580's. His legend as discover of the "New World" is culturally biased, and he should be remembered instead for his colossal navigational failure.

Julius Caesar was one of the foremost military leaders the world has ever known. He helped expand Rome through conquest yet the Roman Empire was not actually created until years after his death, after the numerous civil wars that ravaged Rome were put to an end, emanating in no small part from the total disregard for authority that Julius Caesar displayed on many an occasion. It was this cavalier attitude that may have caused the legendary betrayal resulting in his untimely murder.

William Shakespeare is considered by many to be the single finest writer who ever lived. It has been estimated that more words in the English language are attributed to him than any other writer. Without the support of Queen Elizabeth though, Shakespeare may have toiled in anonymity. There is also the ongoing debate as to whether or not William Shakespeare actually lived, or if it was merely a pseudonym. A number of interesting figures have been offered, including Christopher Marlowe, Edward de Vere and Francis Bacon, due to the mysterious anomalies that nothing in Shakespeare's actual hand exists, not a single word was written about him until years after his death and the biography of the man whose words changed the world was not first written until 1709, almost one hundred years after his alleged death, which also has been the subject of debate.

Ghengis Khan made an ambitious attempt to conquer the world, yet during his reign his empire was basically restricted to Northern and parts of Central Asia, the Upper Middle East and the Southern outskirts of Russia. Khan never reached mainland Europe, as Alexander had reached Asia. The Mongol Empire continued after Ghengis died, yet it was his leadership that allowed it to initially flourish. Due to his barbaric ways there was no chance of a cross-cultural exchange of ideas and principles, such as occurred with Alexander and other imperialistic conquerors.

George Washington was the first President of the United States, yet his appointment was largely cosmetic, as he was not overly active within the actual framing of the new Government. It is as a military general, leading America to victory in the Revolutionary War where his essential mark was made, yet Washington does not rank in military stature alongside Napoleon, Alexander the Great or others such as Ghengis Khan or Julius Caesar. It is an extremely ethnocentric viewpoint that has allowed Washington to rise to such lofty heights among history's most significant figures.

Two other Presidents of the United States often rank on lists such as this one, Thomas Jefferson and Abraham Lincoln. Known as the principal author of the Constitution, Jefferson's ideas, molded with the help of such men as James Madison and Alexander Hamilton, were almost wholly derived from the principles of constitutional democracy developed by John Locke in the late 17th century. Another major milestone for Jefferson, the Louisiana Purchase, was much more of a necessity for Napoleon than it was for Jefferson, who so happened to greatly benefit from the French monarch's monumental economic blunder.

Abraham Lincoln is known as the man who freed the slaves. His early career was far more important, working as a lawyer all the way up through the political ranks until reaching the highest office in the land, during one of the most tumultuous times in American history. His Emancipation Proclamation, which made it illegal to own slaves, tore the country in half, leading in part to the creation of a bipartisan political system, which still exists today. In the years to come, as America continues to degenerate from this political bastardization of what the founding fathers intended Lincoln's actual true significance may eventually be recognized.

Continuing from Lincoln, the civil rights activist Dr. Martin Luther King Jr. could be considered by some as an unnecessary omission. Many came before him, and there were those who continued after him, some continuing to this day. His idea of peaceful activism derives from the teachings of Mohandas Gandhi, and most would argue that Dr. King, while absolutely right in his views, failed to succeed in teaching an unwilling society that all men are created equal, yet they all have the potential to act in such a way that makes them less than equal.

Mohandas Gandhi helped liberate India from British rule in the 1940's, working originally as a lawyer, then as a pacifistic activist. The key to Gandhi's significance is that India, as a country and an empire, has not made impressive strides with their independence, such as other countries have when shedding the yoke of a colonizing empire. Important to note is that the nonviolent activism executed by Gandhi and followed up by Dr. King, was originally proposed as a method of protest by Henry David Thoreau in his landmark work *Civil Disobedience.*

Rene Descartes could have become one of the most brilliant scientific and philosophical minds of his time, if not for his adherence to the stringent archaic religious practices, enforced by the Catholic Church. "I think, therefore I am", Descartes most celebrated quote, unfortunately is not practiced by the majority today, thus seriously reducing his overall significance.

Josef Stalin was responsible for the deaths of over 30 million people and was a large part of the reason why Adolf Hitler was not successful in conquering all of Eastern Europe, yet the climate of Russia, similar to what eventually doomed Napoleon in 1812, may have been far more of a factor than Stalin's leadership. He was a megalomaniacal menace the likes of Hussein, Amin, Ceausescu and Khomeini yet maniacal ideas and actions alone do not warrant a high ranking on this list.

There are many others who have not been mentioned yet warrant at least a brief explanation of why they were excluded. The Wright Brothers were not the first people to achieve flight, with that distinction belonging to a 1783 hot air balloon flight in Paris, France. The design of the airplane, or air glider, was actually created four centuries earlier by Da Vinci.

Alexander Graham Bell invented the telephone, yet it is not widely known that he barely beat another inventor to the patent office, who had invented a similar apparatus to Bell's. What is also not widely known is that it was Thomas Edison who made fundamental improvements to the telephone, which are somewhat responsible for its initial boom in usage.

Three artists, Michelangelo Buonarroti, Pablo Picasso and Wolfgang Amadeus Mozart generally crack lists such as these. The sculptor and painter of the Sistine Chapel was said to have been divinely inspired, yet debate over the appropriateness of his most famous sculpture still exists. One would think that divine intervention would have facilitated no need for such uproar within the religious community, a prime example of selective spirituality. Pablo Picasso is widely considered the greatest artist who ever lived, yet while art may be inspiring to some, transporting the viewer to a better time and place, the chiasm between organized or sometimes disorganized paint on a canvas and concepts such as freedom, democracy and liberty are enormous. Mozart, or Beethoven if you prefer, falls under the same above comparison. Music and art can lift ones spirits, yet ideals are of far greater consequence.

A group of other famous figures would include Thomas Aquinas, Socrates, Joan of Arc, Marie Curie, Charlemagne, Oliver Cromwell, Sigmund Freud and Henry Ford. Tough choices had to be made and the above selections were unfortunately excluded from the finished list. As purely famous figures top the register for noteworthy omissions, there are those in history who just barely got cut, and that most people know absolutely nothing about.

The English Priest John Wyclif led the first reformation against the unsavory rule of the Roman Catholic Church in the 14th century, almost two-hundred years prior to Luther's Protestant reformation that ultimately succeeded. Wyclif was followed by a Bohemian theologian named Jan Hus, yet that second reformation also failed, both needing something as imperative as the printing press for the actual ideas to reach the masses before they could be stamped out by the long arm of the Catholic Church.

Nikolaus August Otto was a German inventor who constructed the first working internal combustion engine, used to help the automobile and aviation industries emerge as a dominant mode of transportation.

Gais Plinius Secundus, known as Pliny the Elder, completed a work titled *Natural History*, where he sources over two thousand ancient texts. This book acts as an encyclopedia of all known branches of science, artistic endeavors and Pliny's own interpretations on humanity and morals. It is perhaps one of the most important all encompassing books ever written, and the only one to survive that bears his name.

The English political philosopher Thomas Hobbes preached an idea known as absolutism, in his 16th century landmark work titled *Leviathan*. It is this work that inspired the emergence of Communism and Fascism, arguing that the individual owes complete obedience to the sovereign. This tenet became bastardized by rulers such as Hitler and Mao Zedong.

Aristarchus of Samos was the first scientist to hypothesize the idea that the Earth revolved around the Sun, yet Aristotelian and Ptolemaic geo-centric astronomy became endorsed by the Catholic Church in the 1st and 2nd century A.D., allowing Aristarchus' correct astronomical views to be discarded and forgotten.

Ganger Hrolf, known as Rollo the Viking, was a marauding Scandinavian raider who eventually settled in Normandy and made a pact with the French ruler Charles the Simple, exchanging his allegiance for land. This became one of the earliest, if not the earliest, forms of feudalism that kept the Middle Ages stagnant, but would eventually lead to uprisings and an early form of democracy, the writing of the Magna Carta.

The Indian Emperor Asoka may be single handedly responsible for the spread of Buddhism, foregoing all further military conquests, focusing on building his empire from within. Asoka has been given the title of the world's first "enlightened" ruler, as his rule was based upon principles of peace during a time of rampant conquest and rebellion.

In the 11th century, a Chinese man named Pi Cheng was the first man to print a document using letters, inventing the first movable type of printing using wooden blocks. Ashurbanipal, a 7th century B.C. King of Assyria may have created the first organized library. The tablets uncovered from his palace at Ninevah are housed in the British Museum in London. Dionysius Exiguous, known as Dennis the Short, was a 6th century monk who created our current system of dating, counting back to his incorrect interpretation of the birth of Jesus of Nazareth.

If it were not for Gavrilo Princip, an eighteen year old Serbian terrorist who murdered Austrian Archduke Franz Ferdinand, both World War I and the Russian Revolution may never have occurred. While World War I is in the discussion, the famous book by Alfred T. Mahan, *The Influence of Sea Power upon History*, led nations to seriously develop their navies, which in turn had a lasting impact into what would turn into World War I.

Two unknown scholars, Jewish philosopher Moses ibn Maimon, also known as Maimonides, and Persian philosopher Ibn Rushd, known as Averroes, both preached and saved the works of Aristotle, in turn helping to further the transition from the Dark Ages into the Age of Reason.

The author Rachel Carson's 1962 book *Silent Spring* helped start the environmental movement. French nobleman Baron Pierre de Coubertin established the modern Olympic Games in 1896, which has been used for everything from protest to terrorist activity to political suppression to basic competition among nothing more than human beings. Spanish explorer Gonzalo Jiminez de Quesada was responsible for returning to Europe with the potato, a crop that could feed entire families, most notably used in Ireland, allowing them to support themselves off other crops.

Hundreds of other no-names go unrecognized for their spectacular deeds. A few more are the Belgian anatomist Andreas Vesalius, the Jewish philosopher Baruch Spinoza, the English naval Captain John Hawkins, scourge of the slave trade and others just like them. These names go unnoticed in history, passed over for the bigger names, yet their contributions are no less important. Can anyone tell me who Norman Borlaug is? Probably not but you might want to know that as of current estimation this man has saved close to one billion lives, but most scholars find him much less influential, important or even significant as Johann Sebastian Bach or Charles Dickens.

It is crucial to understand that a list such as this, while subjective, should serve as a guideline for the future gain of knowledge. The men and women discussed within this book, whether they made the top 50 list or not, should continue to be discussed. That is the sole purpose of this book, debate and discussion. Share your own ideas, with friends and colleagues, with your children and relatives or with whomever you choose. If one person gains knowledge from the writing of this book then a goal is achieved. It is not however, the only goal. The ultimate goal would be to supply knowledge and provide a forum for debate for thousands, or even optimistically millions of people who choose to use their brains and ability to reason, neo-Aristotelian, rather than the alternative.

BIBLIOGRAPHY

Baker, G. P. *Constantine the Great: And the Christian Revolution* (2001)

Bothamley, Jennifer. *Dictionary of Theories* (1993)

Brecht, Bertolt. *Life of Galileo* (1994)

Browne, Janet E. *Charles Darwin: Voyaging* (1996)

Canning, John. *100 Great Kings, Queens and Rulers of the World* (1968)

Chunli, Qu. *The Life of Confucius* (1996)

Da Costa Andrade, Edward Neville. *Rutherford and the Nature of the Atom* (1964)

Dickinson, A. W. *James Watt: Craftsman and Engineer* (1936)

Douglas, David C. *William the Conqueror* (1964)

Downs, Robert B. *Books That Changed The World* (1983)

Fines, John. *Who's Who in the Middle Ages* (1970)

Fox, Robin Lane. *Alexander the Great* (1994)

Fry, Plantagenet Somerset. *1000 Great Lives* (1985)

Goodrick-Clarke, Nicholas. *Paracelsus: Essential Readings* (1999)

Gottlieb, Agnes, Gottlieb, Henry, Bowers, Barbara, Bowers, Brent. *1,000 Years, 1,000 People* (1998)

Grum, Bernard. *The Timetables of History: The New Third Revised Edition* (1991)

Hammontree, Marie. *Albert Einstein: Young Thinker* (1986)

Hart, Michael H. *The 100: A Ranking of the Most Influential Persons in History* (1992)

Hunter, Dard. *Old Papermaking in China and Japan* (1932)

Inati, Shams. *Ibn Sina and Mysticism* (1996)

Josephson, Matthew. *Edison: A Biography* (1992)

Larner, John. *Marco Polo and the discovery of the World* (1999)

Maddicott, J. R. *Simon de Montfort* (1996)

McClellan, James E. and Dorn, Harold. *Science and Technology in World History* (1999)

McLynn, Frank. *Napoleon* (2002)

Morris, Christopher W. *The Social Contract Theorists* (1999)

Nohl, Frederick. *Luther: Biography of a Reformer* (2003)

Norita, Kiyofusa. *A Life of Ts'ai Lung and Japanese Paper Making* (1954)

Pacey, Arnold. *Technology in World History: A Thousand-Year History* (1991)

Paparchontis, Kathleen. *100 World Leaders Who Shaped World History* (2001)

Petersen, William. *Malthus: Founder of Modern Demography* (1998)

Powicke, F. Maurice. *King Henry and the Lord Edward* (1947)

Powicke, F. Maurice. *The Thirteenth Century: 1216 – 1307* (1953)

Reichenbach, Hans. *From Copernicus to Einstein* (1980)

Romm, James. *Herodotus* (1998)

Simmons, John. *The Scientific 100* (1996)

Smith, Linda Wasmer. *Louis Pasteur: Disease Fighter* (1997)

Stanley, Diane. *Saladin: Noble Prince of Islam* (2002)

Thiel, J. H. *Studies in Ancient History* (1994)

Tiner, John Hudson. *100 Scientists Who Shaped World History* (2000)

Toland, John. *Adolf Hitler: The Definitive Biography* (1991)

Waite, Arthur Edward. *Hermetic and Alchemical Writings of Paracelsus, Part 1* (2002)

Wheen, Francis. *Karl Marx: A Life* (2000)

White, Lynn Townsend. *Medieval Technology and Social Change* (1966)

White, Michael. *Isaac Newton: Discovering Laws That Govern the Universe* (1999)

Wilson, David. *Rutherford: Simple Genius* (1984)

Yenne, Bill. *100 Men Who Shaped World History* (1994)

Yount, Lisa. *Antoine Lavoisier: Founder of Modern Chemistry* (1997)

INDEX

218

THE 50 MOST SIGNIFICANT INDIVIDUALS
IN RECORDED HISTORY

1. ARISTOTLE	26. JOHN LOCKE
2. LOUIS PASTEUR	27. SHIH HUANG TI
3. JOHANNES GUTENBURG	28. ADAM SMITH
4. AMENHOTEP IV	29. JAMES CLERK MAXWELL
5. ISAAC NEWTON	30. PLATO
6. SAUL OF TARSUS	31. SARGON THE GREAT
7. JESUS OF NAZARETH	32. THOMAS MALTHUS
8. GALILEO GALILEI	33. ELIZABETH I
9. CHARLES DARWIN	34. ODO DE LAGERY
10. MOHAMMED	35. IGNAC SEMMELWEIS
11. ARCHIMEDES	36. ADOLF HITLER
12. CONSTANTINE I	37. SIDDHARTHA GAUTAMA
13. NICOLAUS COPERNICUS	38. JUSTINIAN I
14. SOLON	39. KONG QIU ZHONGNI
15. ANTOINE LAVOISIER	40. JOHN STUART MILL
16. ALBERT EINSTEIN	41. ERATOSTHENES
17. TSAI LUN	42. LEONARDO DA VINCI
18. MARTIN LUTHER	43. KARL MARX
19. NAPOLEON BONAPARTE	44. YUSEF SALAH ED-DIN
20. ALEXANDER THE GREAT	45. PARACELSUS
21. HAMMURABI	46. ALARIC I
22. WILLIAM THE CONQUEROR	47. JAMES WATT
23. HERODOTUS	48. IBN SINA
24. THOMAS EDISON	49. ERNEST RUTHERFORD
25. MARCO POLO	50. SIMON DE MONTFORT

Printed in the United States
27830LVS00005B/187-309